About this Book

Why is this topic important?

An enormous amount of time and money is being invested in developing executives today. Over the past 20 years, corporations have dedicated more and more resources to ensuring that they have the executive talent to execute their strategy and win in the marketplace. According to our experience working with about half of the Fortune 100 and other leading companies around the world, custom-designed, in-company executive/leadership development programs are a primary means of developing executives. Our 2004 survey of "Global 500" companies indicates that this will continue to be the case over the next two to three years (see the Survey results in Chapter 1). The questions that need to be asked, and which this book addresses, are: How do you create executive development strategies and programs that have real impact? And what are the strategic uses of executive development that companies have found to have significant impact? While many books have been written about leadership development, this book deals particularly with the development of executives.

What can you achieve with this book?

Our goal in writing this book is to help you and your organization achieve your strategic objectives through the use of executive development strategies, systems and programs. This book will provide you with a greater understanding of how best to leverage your investments in executive development. We'll explain the five uses of executive development that have the most business impact, and how they are designed, developed, deployed and measured. You will also learn about executive development "best practices" and what the key trends are likely to be in the field over the next few years.

How is this book organized?

This book is divided into four parts. Chapter 1 summarizes the key trends in executive development, based on a survey of 101 major corporations. Chapter 2 will be useful to the reader interested in learning about the process of creating high-impact executive development strategies, systems and programs linked to your marketplace challenges and business strategy. It describes in detail a five-step process. We also describe in the appendix a Rapid-Cycle Design® process for building line ownership and speeding the time to market of new executive development efforts.

Chapters 3–8 describe the five high-impact uses of executive development. Chapter 3 is an overview of the five, with a brief description of each. Chapters 4–8 present case histories with detailed stories from actual companies' experiences with executive development programs.

Each of these chapters covers one of the five high-impact uses of executive development. The reader is shown the details of why these companies created their executive development strategy, system or program; how they did it; what their process or program looked like; who was involved; and the results they achieved.

Chapter 9, we hope, will convince you that executive development should be part of your overall business strategy. It deals with the elusive issue of metrics. We present mini-case histories showing how various companies have measured the impact of their executive development efforts on individual executive performance and/or business performance. We also summarize in Appendix J the various methods used by these companies for measuring business impact.

If you are interested in improving the development of the executive talent in your organization, this book can assist you in understanding how to get the most from your investment. Literally billions are spent by organizations on teaching their executives to be better leaders and more brilliant stewards of the bottom line. But none of us has unlimited resources—we need to know precisely how to invest in executive development to leverage our investments.

About Pfeiffer

Pfeiffer serves the professional development and hands-on resource needs of training and human resource practitioners and gives them products to do their jobs better. We deliver proven ideas and solutions from experts in HR development and HR management, and we offer effective and customizable tools to improve workplace performance. From novice to seasoned professional, Pfeiffer is the source you can trust to make yourself and your organization more successful.

Essential Knowledge Pfeiffer produces insightful, practical, and comprehensive materials on topics that matter the most to training and HR professionals. Our Essential Knowledge resources translate the expertise of seasoned professionals into practical, how-to guidance on critical workplace issues and problems. These resources are supported by case studies, worksheets, and job aids and are frequently supplemented with CD-ROMs, websites, and other means of making the content easier to read, understand, and use.

Essential Tools Pfeiffer's Essential Tools resources save time and expense by offering proven, ready-to-use materials—including exercises, activities, games, instruments, and assessments—for use during a training or team-learning event. These resources are frequently offered in looseleaf or CD-ROM format to facilitate copying and customization of the material.

Pfeiffer also recognizes the remarkable power of new technologies in expanding the reach and effectiveness of training. While e-hype has often created whizbang solutions in search of a problem, we are dedicated to bringing convenience and enhancements to proven training solutions. All our e-tools comply with rigorous functionality standards. The most appropriate technology wrapped around essential content yields the perfect solution for today's on-the-go trainers and human resource professionals.

www.pfeiffer.com

Essential resources for training and HR professionals

Strategic Executive Development

Strategic Executive Development

The Five Essential Investments

James F. Bolt, Michael McGrath,
and Michael Dulworth

www.pfeiffer.com

Published by Jossey-Bass
A Wiley Imprint
989 Market Street, San Francisco, CA 94103-1741   www.josseybass.com

Jossey-Bass books and products are available through most bookstores. To contact Jossey-Bass directly call our Customer Care Department within the U.S. at 800-956-7739, outside the U.S. at 317-572-3986, or fax 317-572-4002.

Jossey-Bass also publishes its books in a variety of electronic formats. Some content that appears in print may not be available in electronic books.

Library of Congress Cataloging-in-Publication Data

Bolt, James F.
    Strategic executive development: the five essential investments / James F. Bolt, Michael Dulworth, and Michael McGrath.—1st ed.
        p. cm.
    Includes index.
    ISBN-13 978-0-7879-7463-3 (alk. paper)
    ISBN-10 0-7879-7463-3 (alk. paper)
    1. Executives—Training of. I. Dulworth, Mike, 1962- II. McGrath, Michael, 1955- III. Title.
HD30.4.B65 2005
658.4'07124—dc22   2005000722

Printed in the United States of America
FIRST EDITION
HB Printing   10 9 8 7 6 5 4 3 2 1

Contents

Introduction

For twenty-three years we have had the privilege of working with leading companies around the world to support them in their efforts to leverage their investments in executive development. That accumulated experience has resulted in this book. This introduction is provided to help you get the most value from the book. It covers who will get the most out of reading it, defines our terms, describes how the book will benefit you and your organization, and concludes with some information about our organization, Executive Development Associates, Inc.

Who Should Read this Book

Strategic Executive Development: The Five Essential Investments is for senior human resource and learning officers (vice presidents or heads of human resources, chief learning officers, heads of learning and development, vice presidents of training and development, vice presidents and directors of executive and leadership development, talent and talent management development, organization development, and so on) who are concerned with leveraging their investments in executive talent development for maximum impact and with having the executive capabilities and *benchstrength* necessary to achieve their business strategy and win in the marketplace.

Defining Terms

For the purposes of this book, executives and leaders are defined as those who fall into one or more of the following groups:

- *Members of the board of directors:* The chairman of the board, the chief executive officer, the chief operating officer, the president and all elected officers
- *Corporate vice presidents (including functional heads):* Heads or presidents of groups, divisions, business units, or profit centers and their direct reports; all the people included in your executive compensation program
- *High-potential managers:* Managers who have been identified as having the potential to fill an executive-level position in the future

When we use the term *development,* it encompasses any activity aimed at broadening executives' knowledge and experience and enhancing their capabilities.

How this Book Will Benefit You and Your Organization

Strategic Executive Development provides the following:

- A time-tested framework for developing high-impact executive development strategies, systems, and programs that will help you achieve your business strategy and win in the marketplace
- The most current information on where executive development stands in the corporate world today, what approaches are working, and what will be relevant in the next several years
- Insights into how to get the most leverage from your investments, through in-depth case studies on the five high-impact uses of executive development
- Clear evidence of the business impact of corporate executive development, and proven examples for ways companies have measured and validated the impact of executive development

About Executive Development Associates

Since 1982 Executive Development Associates, Inc. (EDA) has pioneered and been a leader in creating custom-designed executive development strategies, systems, and programs that help clients achieve their strategic objectives and win in the marketplace. We work in partnership with clients to make their executive development efforts successful by ensuring maximum leverage and bottom-line results. We have worked with over half of the Fortune 100 and many other leading organizations around the world.

Our mission is to ensure that each client's executive talent is a source of competitive advantage. We accomplish this by

- Creating high-impact, custom-designed executive education strategies, systems and programs
- Developing customized talent management strategies and integrated systems
- Supporting the success and effectiveness of executives through powerful communities of practice peer-to-peer networks
- Conducting research that advances the state of the art and is also practical and immediately applicable

EDA has offices in San Francisco, California, and in New York City.

Strategic Executive Development

CHAPTER ONE

CRITICAL TRENDS IN EXECUTIVE DEVELOPMENT: WHAT LIES AHEAD?

O ur thinking about executive development must be placed in the context of the critical forces and trends shaping the field. Rather than relying on our opinions alone, we'll begin by presenting key findings from our most recent survey of major corporations, including their predictions about the next few years.

Background

We have been conducting trends research on executive development issues since 1983. For our 2004 survey, we formed an advisory board comprising executive development professionals from major companies such as Xerox, Dell, and IBM (see Appendix A for a full listing and biographies of the 2004 Trends Survey Advisory Board).

The Advisory Board assisted us by reviewing and analyzing the survey results, helping us determine the most important findings and implications, and copresenting the findings of the survey results at EDA Network meetings and other key forums. (EDA organizes and facilitates communities of practice, peer-to-peer networks for senior executive leadership development professionals, chief learning officers, heads of talent management, senior HR officers, and other executives.)

In 2004, we also expanded the sample of companies surveyed. Previously the survey was distributed to our database of the most senior executive development and learning professionals; this time, we distributed the survey to our database and the Global 500. We received 101 survey responses. (See Appendix B for a breakdown of respondent demographics.)

Core Trends Survey Questions

The following questions were posed in the Executive Development 2004 Trends Survey:

- What are the conditions that will most influence your executive development efforts over the next two to three years?
- What will be the key objectives of your executive development efforts in the next two to three years?
- What topics will receive the most emphasis in your executive development programs in the next two to three years?
- What policy and strategy activities within the executive development function will be highly emphasized?
- What planning and needs analysis methods will be highly emphasized?
- What program design and development activities will be highly emphasized?
- What learning methods will be emphasized most?
- In which best practices does your organization excel?
- What percentage of each of the following executive populations will participate in formal executive development activities over the next two to three years? How many days per year, and what development activities will they be most likely to participate in?
  - The chief executive officer, all elected officers, and the senior or executive management team
  - Corporate vice presidents (including functional heads), heads and presidents of groups, divisions, business units, or profit centers, and their direct reports
  - High-potential managers—managers who have been identified as having the potential to fill an executive-level position in the future

Research Findings Highlights

As you read the highlights from this revealing survey, you might want to be thinking about the implications for you and your organization.

Conditions Influencing Executive Development

The survey began with this question: what are the highly influential conditions that will impact executive development in companies during the next two to three years? The answer, overwhelmingly, was "lack of benchstrength." Over 70 percent of the companies that responded are worried about the breadth and depth of their executive talent and are beginning to understand that shifting workforce demographics will put even more pressure on this issue in the future. In addition, over 50 percent of the respondents cited changing business strategies, increased competition, the need for increased collaboration across the organization, and globalization as key factors driving their executive development efforts.

It is also interesting to note which conditions garnered a low percentage of responses, including these:

- New information technology – 11.9 percent
- Downsizing – 7.9 percent
- Increased need for awareness around corporate responsibility – 6.9 percent
- Political unrest (e.g., terrorist threats and acts) – 5.0 percent

Some of the major events of the last few years—for example, the e-commerce, dot-com, and technology boom of the 1990s; the global recession; the wave of

Figure 1.1. Highly Influential Conditions on Executive Leadership Development.

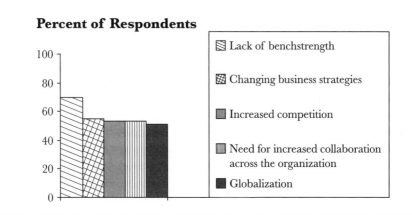

Percent of Respondents

- Lack of benchstrength
- Changing business strategies
- Increased competition
- Need for increased collaboration across the organization
- Globalization

Source: © Executive Development Associates, Inc., 2004.

corporate scandals; and the September eleventh attacks and the subsequent "war on terrorism"—seem to have had little lasting effect on most corporations, according to the Trends Survey responses.

It is obvious that the current business environment is very intense, fast-moving, and extremely competitive, resulting in shifting business strategies that must be executed quickly and efficiently. This situation places extreme pressure on the top executives of companies and quickly brings to light any misalignment between existing executive capabilities and the capabilities needed to execute a company's business strategy.

Besides the hiring of new people, the use of executive development programs, processes, and systems is one of the only alternatives available to quickly "retool" the executive ranks so their capabilities are aligned with those required to execute a new business strategy and succeed in the global marketplace.

The number one objective for corporate executive development efforts, far ahead of all others, is "Increase benchstrength/ensure replacements for key jobs or people" (80 percent). Also, companies seem committed to closing the talent gap they expect to experience at the executive level by focusing on processes aimed at accelerating the development of their pool of high-potential talent. Running a close second to this objective for executive development was "Accelerate the development of high-potentials" (63 percent).

Figure 1.2 lists the respondents' top five key objectives for executive development efforts in the next two to three years.

In Chapter Six we'll describe two company case studies that illustrate innovative approaches to accelerating the development of high potentials.

Figure 1.2. Key Objectives.

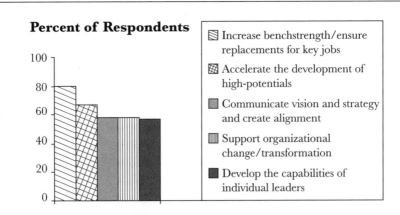

Source: © Executive Development Associates, Inc., 2004.

The Most Important Executive Development Topics

The focus on imparting "soft" skills more than "hard" skills through executive development programs is evident in Figure 1.3. The top three areas of emphasis—"Leadership," "Leading/Managing Change," and "Managing Human Performance"—are all typically characterized as soft skills; hard skills such as "Business Acumen" and "Financial Management" were scored lower. But overall, there is a good balance in the emphases placed on both soft- and hard-skill areas in executive development efforts.

One of our advisory board members observed that the top ten topics broke down into two equal categories: head skills and heart skills. Head skills—that is, business capabilities—include the following:

- Strategy execution
- Business acumen
- Financial management
- General management skills
- Globalization

Heart skills—that is, leadership capabilities—include the following:

- Leadership (envisioning, enrolling, and empowering)
- Leading/managing organizational change
- Managing human performance
- Developing others
- Interpersonal skills

Figure 1.3. Topics That Will Receive the Most Emphasis.

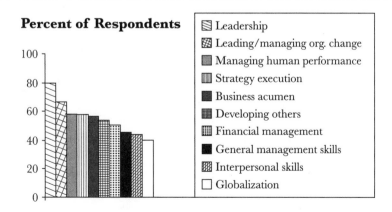

Source: © Executive Development Associates, Inc., 2004.

It is no surprise to us that leadership is the number one topic; it has been since we started our Trends Survey in 1983. It is surprising, however, given the current business trend of focusing on growth—especially on internally generated growth versus growth through acquisitions—that entrepreneurship/intrapreneurship and innovation are not ranked as major areas of emphasis for the next two to three years.

In the case studies in Chapters Four through Eight you will see that most of the high-impact uses of executive development described have a balance of the leadership and business topics/capabilities emphasized in the survey.

Executive Development Policy and Strategy, Needs Assessment, Design and Development, and Delivery

The second major section of the Trends Survey focused on the design, development, and deployment of executive development strategy, systems, processes, and programs.

Policy and Strategy

The key trend highlighted in Figure 1.4 is that companies plan to integrate all aspects of their executive development efforts into a holistic process and system, getting

Figure 1.4. Policy and Strategy Activities That Will Be Emphasized.

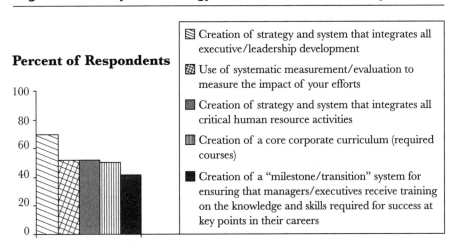

Source: © Executive Development Associates, Inc., 2004.

away from perceiving executive education as a stand-alone program. This integrated approach includes such areas as high-potential identification and development, succession planning, on-the-job development, experiences, mentoring/coaching, and executive education (internal and external programs). The Leadership Institute of UBS (see case study in Chapter Four) is an excellent example of an integrated system.

Planning and Needs Analysis

When we asked how companies are planning their executive development efforts, 81 percent of respondents said top management requests and suggestions were the most cited source of information, 70 percent used 360-degree feedback data (360-degree feedback is feedback from multiple involved parties, such as an individual's manager, peers, and those who work for them), and 58 percent used analysis of aggregate talent review results of the target population (see Figure 1.5). Finally, the use of assessment surveys or structured interviews with prospective participants to identify needs was chosen by only 54.5 percent of the respondents. Notice that the focus seems to be on *reactive* ways to identify needs (such as use of top management's requests and suggestions) rather than careful, systematic analysis (360-degree data, formal needs assessments, and the like). We don't suggest that the requests and suggestions of top management should be disregarded—interviews with top management are usually a key part of any quality needs

Figure 1.5. Planning and Needs Analysis
Activities That Will Be Emphasized.

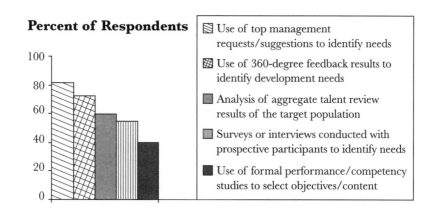

Source: © Executive Development Associates, Inc., 2004.

assessment process—but we are saying that executive development systems solely based upon these requests and suggestions may be off the mark.

Chapter Two presents a foolproof process for developing new executive development strategies, systems, and programs that directly support your business strategy and objectives, including the all-important needs assessment step.

Design and Development

Figure 1.6 shows that over 70 percent of responding companies will use external consultants to assist with the design and development of their executive development programs. Many of our advisory board and network members seem to think the expected increase in the use of external consultants is due to a decrease in their internal capacity and capabilities caused by staff reductions over recent years.

Learning Methods

The use of senior executives as faculty in executive development programs is a strong trend; over 75 percent of respondents said that this will be a primary learning method utilized (see Figure 1.7). This is the first time since we began conducting the survey in 1983 that using company executives as faculty has been

Figure 1.6. Program Design and Development Activities That Will Be Emphasized.

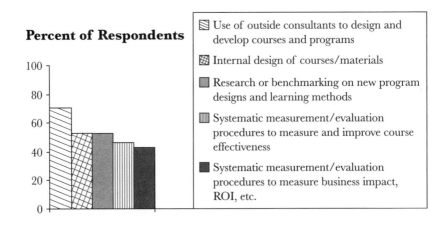

Source: © Executive Development Associates, Inc., 2004.

number one on the list of learning methods. This is supported by our consulting work, in which we see more and more clients relying on their top executives to actually teach content rather than to simply make cameo appearances to kick off or close programs. Closely following this method is action learning, which is used by 73 percent of the respondents. This method puts participants together in teams to work on real, current and pressing business challenges, with the goal of improving the business and developing executives. The projects worked on by the Action Learning Teams are almost always "sponsored" by senior executives.

The composition of the project team provides learning opportunities for the membership. The educational component of Action Learning has clear goals for development and learning—for both individuals and the team—structured into the process. What is perhaps most significant about Action Learning is that participants are able to immediately apply what they learn to real work.

More traditional learning methods, such as the use of outside faculty experts and outside speakers, continue to be widely utilized, by 63 percent and 67 percent, respectively. Another prominent learning method is the use of external executive coaches, reported by 56 percent of respondents. Internal coaches are used much less frequently, by 32 percent of respondents.

It is also interesting to note that despite all the hype about Web-based and computer-based learning methods, these are utilized by only 34 percent of companies in executive development programs.

Figure 1.7. Learning Methods.

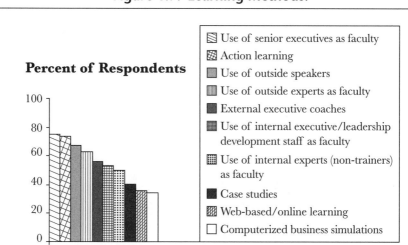

Source: © Executive Development Associates, Inc., 2004.

Executive Development Best Practices

EDA listed twelve "best practices" that we identified in our work with large organizations and asked the respondents to self-assess on these items (see Figure 1.8). They were asked to choose each practice at which they excelled (see Appendix C for definitions of the twelve best practices).

The number-one best practice, chosen by over 69 percent of the respondents, was the custom design of executive development programs. *Custom designed programs* are defined as "programs that address a company's unique, specific challenges and opportunities and help create or drive vision, values, and strategies."(Chapter Two presents a proven process for you to use to create such custom-designed executive/ leadership development strategies, systems, and programs.)

The second-highest-rated best practice was the alignment of executive development to business strategy, with 64.9 percent of respondents choosing this practice. Chapter Two also covers the process for "linking to strategy."

The following best practices rounded out the top five:

- Top management-driven (63.9 percent): Our top executives champion our executive development efforts. We have a senior, line-executive advisory board. Our top executives attend the programs as participants and also teach when appropriate.

Figure 1.8. Best Practices at Which Your Organization Excels.

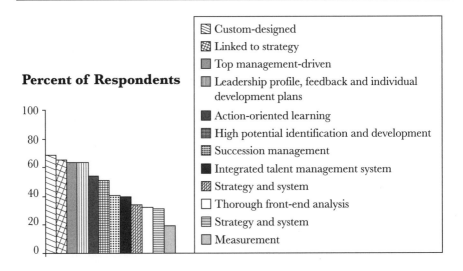

Source: © Executive Development Associates, Inc., 2004.

- Leadership profile, feedback, and individual development plans (63.9 percent): We use a custom-designed (linked to our vision, values, and strategies), multi-rater leadership instrument/inventory to provide confidential development feedback to our executives.
- Action-oriented learning (54.6 percent): Our executive learning experiences are action oriented. Whenever feasible, we use some form of action learning in which participants apply what they have learned to real, current business problems or opportunities.

It is interesting to note that *measurement* was ranked lowest of all of the best practices listed. In various parts of the survey, measurement was identified as a critical component of an executive development effort. Also, companies clearly indicated that they will need to better measure the impact of their development activities on executive effectiveness and business outcomes. Obviously, there continues to be much opportunity for improvement in most companies in this regard.

Chapter Nine deals with how organizations are measuring the business impact of their executive development efforts.

Executive Development by Level

We are often asked whether there are differences in development approaches among the C-level or elected officers, corporate vice presidents, and high-potential managers. Our Trends Survey indicated that there are some significant differences, both in the development methods used at the various levels and the amount of time spent on developmental activities, but perhaps not as much difference as you might expect.

As shown in Figure 1.9, 61.5 percent of C-level executives are expected to participate in executive development activities an average of 8.8 days per year. The main development activities are executive coaching, customized programs developed by external consultants, and customized programs developed by internal staff. The least-used developmental activity is off-the-shelf programs.

As shown in Figure 1.10, 68.6 percent of corporate vice presidents will participate in executive development activities an average of 9.7 days per year. The top development activity is executive coaching, followed by customized programs developed by external consultants and, in a tie for third place, customized programs developed by internal staff and developmental job assignments. The least-used developmental activity is off-the-shelf programs.

As shown in Figure 1.11, 66.1 percent of high-potential managers participate in executive development activities an average of 13.5 days per year. The top development activities are developmental job assignments, customized programs

Figure 1.9. C-Level Executives.

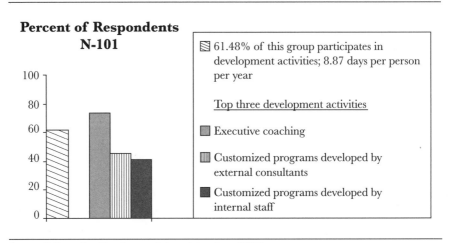

Figure 1.10. Corporate VPs and Heads or Presidents of Groups, Divisions, Business Units, and Profit Centers.

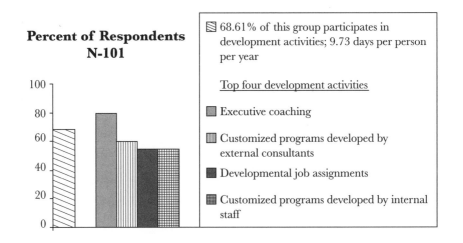

Note: Corporate vice presidents include functional heads; direct reports of all these executives are included.

developed by internal staff, and executive coaching. The least-used developmental activity is participation on external boards.

In summary, the major differences among these three levels exist between the most senior executives and those who have been identified as high potential managers. As the figures show, high-potential managers receive significantly more developmental focus—almost 50 percent more, as measured by the average number of days spent in development activities. They also spend most of their time in developmental job assignments compared with the primary focus on executive coaching for the senior-most executives.

Executive Development 2004 Trends Survey Highlights and Conclusions

Although there are many interesting highlights and conclusions that could be drawn from the survey, there are a few that we think are of special interest.

1. First, increasing benchstrength is the top business condition and objective for the first time in the over-twenty-year history of the Trends Survey. Not only has it jumped up many slots in the rankings, but it is far in front of the next-highest issue. And it has pulled along with it "Accelerating the development of

Figure 1.11. High-Potential Managers.

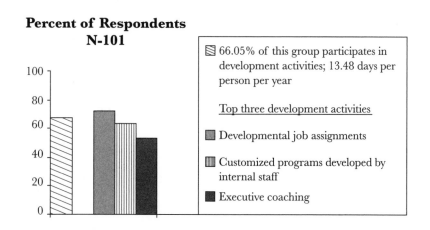

Note: High-potential managers are those who have been identified as having the potential to fill an executive position in the future.

Source: © Executive Development Associates, Inc., 2004.

high potentials" as a primary means of increasing benchstrength. This is clearly a dramatic shift, one that we must pay attention to.

   The company case studies in Chapters Four through Eight all have varying degrees of relevance to the benchstrength challenge facing organizations. The most obvious of these is in Chapter Six, on accelerating the development of emerging leaders; two interesting approaches are presented.

2. We see that communicating vision and creating unity/alignment is a major objective of executive development. This is encouraging, as it reinforces the unmistakable march over the last ten or more years toward a more strategic use of executive development. Gone are the days when our development efforts consisted mostly of sending a few high-potential people off to university executive education programs. Increasingly, organizations are using executive development to build the capabilities they need to achieve their strategic agenda.

   Chapter Four presents a dramatic case study of how both Texas Instruments and UBS use executive development to create unity and alignment around their vision and business strategy.

3. Development of business acumen is a big need, and we include in this category the building of basic business skills. There is a clear recognition that executives' capabilities in these areas are not what they need to be.

   Chapter Eight demonstrates how Weyerhaeuser used its leadership institute to build business acumen in the leaders who are expected to rebuild the company.

4. The use of outside consultants to help with design and development is expected to be high. One of our advisory board members explained that with downsizing of internal staff they just don't have the talent internally anymore and have to use outside consultants.

5. Senior executives serving as faculty, action learning, and coaching will be top learning methods. The big surprise here was that so many companies predicted that the use of their own senior executives would be the most utilized learning method—wow! This outcome jibes with our personal experience and with what we hear from our clients, too. Executive participants in their executive development programs seem to want to hear from their own senior executives.

   Action learning is still seen as a powerful learning method. There seems to be a low tolerance for theoretical learning and a high attraction to learning that is embedded in real work.

   Executive coaching: stand back, folks – it's the Wild West. Is it just the latest fad or the real deal? Time will tell, but for now the survey says it will be used extensively for the very top layers of executives.

6. "Worst" practices: Thorough needs analysis, top-down implementation and measurement. Now, this is troublesome stuff. "Prescription without diagnosis"

is malpractice, isn't it? Yet, thorough needs analysis was not ranked very high in the policy section of the survey; plus, respondents say they aren't very good at needs assessment in the best practices part of the survey. We hope that Chapter Two will be of help to those who want to improve in needs analysis.

Respondents say that in using executive development for organizational change it's too seldom that top management attends first (what happened to role modeling?). Finally, throughout the survey, our 101 respondents said in various ways that use of metrics was going to be a really big deal going forward, yet it is the lowest rated "best practice." In Chapter Nine we explore how several major companies have successfully measured the progress of their executive development programs.

7. Integrated executive development systems will be much more important. It's crystal clear that stand-alone programs and processes won't cut it any longer. We want, and we will need to create and deliver, comprehensive, integrated executive development systems (succession planning, external and internal executive education, leadership development, high-potential identification and development, mentoring, coaching, on-the-job development, and so on) for developing the executive talent our organizations need.

Unfortunately, although we say that integrated executive development systems will be critical, what we are really good at (see the best-practices ratings) is creating custom programs.

The last comparable survey we conducted was four years ago. See Appendix D for a comparison between that survey and the latest, with highlights on the following:

- Business conditions affecting executive development
- Key objectives
- Topics
- Policy and strategy
- Planning and needs analysis
- Program design and development
- Learning activities and methods

Summary

The 2004 Trends Survey was by far the most interesting we have conducted. The survey findings strongly support the need for improvements in measuring the impact of executive development (see Chapter Nine). A critical objective over the next few years will be communicating vision and creating unity and alignment (see Chapter Four). And a major objective for companies will be accelerating the development of high-potential managers or emerging leaders (see Chapter Six).

The biggest challenge facing organizations is building benchstrength. The fact is, most of the five high-impact uses of executive development affect benchstrength. These high-impact uses are detailed in the following chapters:

Chapter Four: Creating Strategic Unity and Alignment. When we do this well, we are building a deep understanding and ownership of the organization, vision, values, and strategy among executives and emerging leaders, which strengthens our current and future leadership.

Chapter Five: Ensuring the Successful Transition of New Executives. When we help newly appointed executives transition into their executive roles quickly and effectively, we reduce failure rates and turnover, and we improve performance, thereby strengthening the bench.

Chapter Six: Accelerating the Development of Emerging Leaders. Obviously, when we find ways to speed up the development of the pool of high-potential managers or emerging leaders who are in the pipeline for our key executive positions, we are most directly affecting benchstrength.

Chapter Seven: Transforming Organizations. In many cases of transformation, executive development is used not only as a catalyst for change but also to build the executive capabilities (mindsets, knowledge, and skills) needed to make the transformation. In such cases we are strengthening the current executive bench and reducing the need to hire from outside.

Chapter Eight: Identifying and Addressing Critical Business Challenges. When an organization is faced with a critical challenge and needs to build new executive capabilities to successfully address that challenge, it is dealing with one form of benchstrength problem (for example, retooling its executive ranks rather than firing and rehiring). The kinds of programs described in Chapter Eight can therefore contribute to building benchstrength.

Next Up:

In the next chapter we will present a proven process for creating custom-designed executive development strategies, systems, and programs that build the executive capabilities needed to achieve our strategic objectives.

CHAPTER TWO

CREATING EXECUTIVE DEVELOPMENT STRATEGIES AND PROGRAMS THAT SUPPORT YOUR BUSINESS OBJECTIVES

In the chapters that follow we describe high-impact uses of executive development and show you how a well-designed and carefully executed program benefits both the organization and the executives who participate. Before you make any investment in executive development, however, we recommend that you become well grounded in the process steps that are crucial to creating high-impact strategies and programs. You want to make sure you have a strategy, process, or program that builds the executive capabilities needed to successfully address your marketplace challenges and execute your strategy. All executive development efforts must be built from a strong, fundamental process if they are to be successful. Otherwise they are too likely to be a waste of time and money—and they may even throw the organization off course.

Even though we custom-design our development strategies, systems, and programs, the process for creating all of them is the same. If these steps are followed with discipline, then the outcome will be of the highest possible quality. Skip steps or take shortcuts, and trouble lurks.

The Five-Step Process

Whether you are building a program yourself or working with a consultant, to have an outstanding outcome with significant, measurable business impact you must take the following five steps (detailed in Table 2.1).

Table 2.1. EDA Five-Step Process.

	Activities	Output
Research and analysis	• Analyze company documents • Interview/survey stakeholders	• Findings and recommendations • Preliminary design of system and program(s)
Design	• Create architecture and blueprint for system and program(s)	• System elements, program theme, objectives, windowpanes, and module objectives
Material development/ faculty sourcing	• Source and prepare faculty for program elements • Develop learning materials	• Integrated faculty team • Participant/faculty materials
Pilot program(s)	• Initial conduct • Test/evaluate	• Required revisions
Continuous improvement	• Ongoing evaluation • Measure impact	• Ongoing improvements

1. Research and analysis (needs assessment)
2. Design
3. Material development and faculty sourcing
4. Pilot program
5. Follow-through and continuous improvement

Step One: Research and Analysis (Needs Assessment)

Our philosophy is that prescription without diagnosis is malpractice. Research and analysis is, without a doubt, the most critical step in the five-step process. Tailoring executive development to a company's business strategy requires a thorough understanding of the organization's business and leadership challenges. You build that understanding by completing these activities:

• Reviewing relevant documents to develop an overall picture of the organization
• Surveying and interviewing executives and key stakeholders
• Interviewing outside experts

Reviewing Relevant Documents to Develop an Overall Picture of the Organization. Review documents that will provide insight and information about:

- Organization history and performance
- Marketplace challenges
- Vision, values, and strategic objectives
- Key goals, and what executives and managers must know and be able to do to meet these goals
- Current management issues, challenges, and opportunities
- Major changes under way in the business environment that require new or modified responses and skills

Appendix E provides a list of recommended documents to gather and review.

Surveying and Interviewing Executives and Key Stakeholders. The goal of this part of research and analysis is to understand major anticipated marketplace challenges and the organization's vision, values, strategies, and priorities. This will also help you acquire a feel for the organization's culture and how it may need to change.

We recommend conducting one-on-one interviews with a sample of the target audience. Larger organizations may also use customized on-line surveys to reach a larger number of executives quickly and economically. The survey and interviews help to uncover the specific capabilities (mindsets, knowledge, and skills, as well as practices, techniques, and behaviors) required for success—today and in the future.

Interviewing Outside Experts. It's important to capture a fresh, unbiased view of the organization through the collective eyes of industry experts, customers, and consultants. This part of the process is helpful in getting a more objective perspective on the organization's opportunities and challenges.

For example, when we interviewed the CEO of Texaco years ago, he suggested that we also interview his strategy consultant—and we did. It was extremely valuable to get an outside view of the challenges facing the organization from an expert in the industry who had firsthand information about Texaco.

Outcomes You Can Expect from the Research and Analysis Step. At the conclusion of your diagnostics in Step One, you should be able to produce and report on the following:

- Key business challenges and prioritized executive development needs (based on gaps between the capabilities we have versus what we will need)

- A draft of an excellent leader profile—a prioritized list of capabilities that executives need to successfully address the most important marketplace challenges, achieve their vision, live their values, and implement their business strategy (the profile often serves as the basis for creating a 360-degree leadership feedback instrument for use later on in the development process)
- A draft long-term plan for executive development, including recommended architecture, strategy, and overall system (system recommendations typically include objectives and design concepts for the development of current executives and for accelerating the development of high-potential leaders)

A widely recognized best practice is to assemble a high-level advisory group—made up of line executives and other key senior executive stakeholders in your company—to advise program designers, ensure relevance, and build ownership throughout the five-step process. We recommend that you brief your advisory group on the research and analysis outcomes to ensure their complete agreement or "buy-in" before you launch Step Two, the design phase.

Step Two: Design

In this second step, the information collected and evaluated in the research and analysis phase is used to develop creative approaches for achieving the objectives developed in Step One. Although the research and analysis step often culminates with a draft design concept, in the design phase we need to create a detailed design document. This step encompasses the overall system theme, objectives, and design of each process and program element in the executive development system.

A successful design must include these elements:

- An explanation of the long-term executive development strategic plan or system, detailing such things as which executives get developed, why, when, where, and how
- Alignment with the organization's vision, values, and strategic objectives, as determined in Step One
- Program and process descriptions, including learning objectives, specific topics to be covered, and proposed learning methods, as well as preliminary faculty recommendations if faculty are involved
- A variety of action learning approaches (see Appendix F for typical action learning activities)
- A strategy to ensure transfer of learning, application, and follow-through; individual participants must be encouraged and supported in applying what they learned to their everyday work environment

The design will provide the basis for a program review with your advisory board.

Step Three: Material Development and Faculty Sourcing

Different executive development programs will have varying degrees of reliance on outside experts to serve as faculty. But in almost all cases experts will need to be engaged to help create materials. If it becomes clear in the execution of Step Two that certain faculty are desired, contact them immediately so they can begin working with the project team on the detailed design of their sessions and the learning, teaching, and program materials that will be required. As we noted in Chapter One, it's becoming more common that your organization's senior executives may be part of the faculty.

Choosing Faculty. The key to choosing faculty is to match the appropriate scholars, consultants, and business executives to the final specifications for the program design. Likewise, your project team should review its strategy, do its research, and determine the best fit. Are you looking for information on cutting-edge industry practices or on general management trends? Do you want the experience of someone who has looked at your industry as a whole, worked with several companies in your industry, or gained specific experience with a competitor? Do you want big-name faculty that your executive will be impressed with (and who tend to be very expensive) or very good but not yet discovered faculty who are harder to find but will perhaps meet your needs just as well? Do you want to use your own executives because they will have credibility and know the company better than outsiders?

Once external faculty have been selected, they must be properly integrated into the development process. You should conduct faculty team meetings at your facilities to help these outside experts fully understand and connect with your senior executives and your company. Typical faculty meetings include the following:

- Briefings by senior company executives on your business and its challenges
- A full review of the research and analysis results (Step One)
- A walk-through of the complete design, with each faculty person reviewing the objectives and learning process of his or her session
- Discussion on how faculty will connect and link to each other's sessions

Whatever method you choose, the goal is to develop a close-knit team that will deliver an integrated, seamless learning experience—rather than a parade of interesting speakers.

Material Development. Of course, the best faculty in the world is ineffective without quality materials. We've all been to training workshops where we are given a telephone-book-sized binder full of charts and lists that will never be looked at again.

In preparing materials, a development team should ask whether their learning and teaching materials do the following:

- Reinforce and communicate the organization's vision, strategic direction, values, and goals
- Address marketplace challenges and strategic objectives
- Develop the executive capabilities required for success
- Use a balanced format emphasizing both conceptual and skill-building aspects of managing and leading
- Present leading-edge concepts and practices
- Emphasize the practical and hard-hitting, representing the real world rather than academic theory

Any program materials that don't meet these criteria should be left out.

Outcomes You Can Expect from Step Three. By the end of your material development and faculty sourcing phase, the following should be complete:

- Assembly of faculty members who have been screened, selected, prepared, and scheduled and are working as a real team
- Selection and scheduling of venue and facilities
- Camera-ready copies of
  - Appropriate preattendance materials
  - In-class participant materials
  - Application exercises and assignment instructions
  - Case studies (if appropriate)
  - Audiovisual materials
  - A personal journal and action-planning guide
- An evaluation process and forms, including customized metrics, if appropriate, to measure business impact
- The follow-through process for supporting and tracking the application of what was learned
- If appropriate, a custom-designed Web site to support participant communications, sharing, networking, and learning before and after classroom events

Step Four: Pilot Program

We're always somewhat reluctant to use the term *pilot program* when referring to executive development. The fact is, there is no pilot, per se—the first program you create is the one by which your efforts will be judged. When you're working with executives, the program had better be right the first time—or there won't be a second time. If you are not confident about running the program with executives, you can try it, or segments of it, with lower-level managers in the organization.

However, to tell the truth, we never do this. We can't emphasize too strongly that if you've faithfully followed this five-step process outlined here, the odds are that you will have a successful initial program.

Your new program or process is now ready to implement. The pilot is a key quality-control tool that will ensure that your executive development program has been rigorously evaluated and meets all your objectives.

Implementation includes the following steps:

- Testing the program or process by conducting it with participants and key stakeholders
- Facilitating the program (for classroom programs, see Appendix G for typical facilitator activities)
- Evaluating the pilot program results
- Revising the design, curriculum, materials, learning methods, and faculty as needed, based on the evaluation results of the pilot program (in our experience, if we've followed every step up to this point in the process, the revisions are minor!)

Step Five: Follow-Through and Continuous Improvement

Once the pilot is complete and fully implemented, do not assume that the process remains static. It's critical to continually refine your program and process in order to maintain the cutting edge you so carefully created. This is accomplished in the following ways:

- Administer participant evaluations at the completion of each session and use them to guide revisions
- Conduct three- to six-month follow-up evaluations to measure application and impact; custom metrics can be created for tracking results if desired
- If you've created a 360-degree leadership inventory, readminister it in the future to measure the improvement in leadership effectiveness over time

- Provide learning transfer and application support and track progress through a follow-through system such as Fort Hill's Friday5s®, a Web-based tool that helps users keep course follow-through and goals a priority and track progress over time[1]

Follow-through and continuous improvement are crucial to maintaining a living program. These also provide the following outcomes:

- Identification of additional development needs and targets for future development
- Regularly presented summaries of evaluations and results for key stakeholders and your advisory board
- Measurement of the impact of your system, programs, and process
- Evidence that what was learned has been applied, and measurement of individual and group progress over time

Executive Development Associates' Rapid-Cycle Design® Process

The five-step process usually takes about six months to complete. Clients have expressed two concerns about this. One is that in some cases the process is too slow, as clients are sometimes under pressure to respond quickly to needs for new executive development strategies and programs. The second concern is that program designers are having trouble securing ownership or buy-in from the company's line management.

We developed our Rapid-Cycle Design Process (RCD) to simultaneously

- Streamline the five-step process, dramatically reducing the time to market for new strategies and programs
- Engage key line executives in a way that results in their ownership of the new executive development strategy and programs

For more information about EDA's Rapid-Cycle Design Process, see Appendix H.

---

1. Fort Hill Company specializes in assisting companies with follow-through systems that increase the return on investment of training and development and business initiatives. http://www.forthillcompany.com.

Summary

In Chapter One we explored the future of executive development by viewing the predictions of major corporations about future objectives, topics, learning methods, strategy, policy, and best practices. In this chapter we presented a foolproof process for creating executive development strategies, systems, and programs linked to your business objectives.

The five-step process clearly identifies the capabilities required to achieve your vision, live your values, and execute critical business strategy.

Next Up

Gaining an understanding of the common, critical issues companies face that can be successfully addressed with executive development will help you optimize your time and financial resources. In Chapter Three, we describe what we believe are the five uses of executive development that companies have found to have the biggest impact; these investments provide the highest strategic value.

CHAPTER THREE

THE FIVE HIGH-IMPACT USES OF EXECUTIVE DEVELOPMENT

In working with leading companies around the world, we've seen good and bad uses of executive development strategies and programs. We've also been able to identify the uses of executive development that seem to yield major payoffs for our clients.

In this chapter, we will outline the five uses of executive development that we believe have the biggest impact:

1. Creating strategic unity and alignment
2. Ensuring the successful transition of new executives
3. Accelerating the development of emerging leaders
4. Transforming the organization
5. Identifying and addressing critical business challenges

If you are thinking about creating a new executive development strategy or program or taking a fresh look at what you already have in place, be sure you consider the five high-impact uses outlined here. If your objectives don't include these, you may not get the most out of your investment in executive development. Also note that company executive development strategies often address more than one of these uses.

Creating Strategic Unity and Alignment

A corporate strategy is useless if most people in your company don't understand or buy into it, or if the managers you expect to implement your strategy do not have the capabilities (that is, the knowledge, mindsets, and skills) to do so. A critical function of executive development is to create unity and alignment around a corporate strategy. We call this *strategic unity.*

Organizations with a high degree of strategic unity have

- A compelling vision, inspiring values, and a winning business strategy
- Deep understanding, ownership, and commitment throughout the organization
- Goals and actions aligned at multiple levels of the organization, including the business unit, the team, and the individual
- People—starting with executives—who are equipped with the capabilities required to achieve the vision, live the values, and execute the strategy

In Chapter Four we demonstrate how Texas Instruments achieved strategic unity and alignment through their "Creating Our Future" workshops, as well as how UBS uses their Leadership Institute to set and achieve their strategic agenda.

Ensuring the Successful Transition of New Executives

With every promotion to a key new management level—especially the executive level—comes a whole new set of capabilities required for success. In many companies, these key transition points include

- Managing other people for the first time
- Managing other managers for the first time
- The first executive-level management position

Failure rates are high when new managers step into these roles without effective preparation and support. In Edward Betof's 1995 book *Just Promoted! How to Survive and Thrive in Your First 12 Months as a Manager,* he points out that approximately 40 percent fail in their first eighteen months. These failure rates apply to all levels of management including newly appointed executives.

When it comes to placing executives in new positions, a trial and error method is simply too time-consuming, painful, and costly. The impact they have on the organization is tremendous. Executive development and preparation are too important to be left to chance.

A sound executive development strategy should identify the critical challenges faced by new executives and create a program and process that will

- Ensure that participants have the capabilities required to perform successfully (covering the common needs of all executives in transition as well as the executives' individual needs)

- Clarify the participant's roles and responsibilities as an executive and leader
- Minimize management error and failure rates
- Ensure understanding of the executive's role in achieving the vision, living the values, executing strategy, and leading change
- Build a sense of total enterprise and teamwork beyond the executive's individual area of responsibility
- Establish working relationships and networks with other transitioning executives—people with whom the executive will need to work effectively in order to succeed
- Demonstrate the organization's commitment to development
- Support the recruitment and retention of executives

We demonstrate in Chapter Five how "Trinity Technology's" New Directors Program (we've given the company a pseudonym, as the original staff we worked with have since left the company) helps the company's newly appointed directors succeed.

Accelerating the Development of Emerging Leaders

One of the biggest worries of CEOs is how to maintain the company's leadership supply. Is the company equipped to run seamlessly after the loss of a key executive? Are there sufficient qualified candidates at the ready to fill key jobs? When an important job becomes vacant, can you always fill it from within if you want to? Is a system in place to ensure that the next generation of executives will be ready to handle the next generation of business challenges? In Chapter One we noted that 80 percent of our survey companies saw benchstrength as their number-one challenge.

Executive development should help accelerate the development of your best talent to ensure you have the benchstrength your organization needs. In Chapter Six we present the process developed for the First Bank of Sweden to accelerate the development of emerging leaders by using an innovative leadership forum. We also present the Accelerated Leadership Program that was used to rapidly develop 175 high-potential executives at "Consolidated Bank" (we've used a pseudonym, as the organization later merged with another bank and no longer exists).

Transforming the Organization

Every organization requires a major transformation at some point. Dramatic external challenges, such as an economic downturn or shifting marketplace, or an acquisition or merger, can shake up everything and everyone. Some forward-thinking leaders drive change before an external crisis forces a reactive, defensive response.

In our experience, executive development forums are a powerful way to support organizational transformation. They act as a catalyst for required change, and they ensure that executives are equipped with the capabilities necessary to lead /or manage the transformation. Executive development solutions help companies through transformations by

- Creating dissatisfaction with the current situation or status quo
- Ensuring deep understanding of the rationale or requirement for change (that is, the "burning platform")
- Providing forums for creating and communicating the vision of the desired future state—in other words, answering the question, "What will it be like when we successfully transform?"—and doing so in a way that results in deep ownership of the vision
- Identifying the critical success factors for making the transformation
- Creating an action plan for the change
- Providing ways to monitor progress, share new knowledge, and modify the plan as needed over time
- Developing the executive leadership capabilities needed to achieve the transformation
- Celebrating success

Chapter Seven shows how Weyerhaeuser used leadership development to catalyze and guide their corporate transformation.

Identifying and Addressing Critical Business Challenges

Every business has a set of important business issues, priorities, opportunities, and challenges. Some are externally focused, such as entering global markets, understanding new customer requirements, or addressing competitive threats. Others are internal challenges, such as becoming more market- or customer-focused, improving time to market, or accelerating new business innovation. Often an issue is both mission-critical and pervasive, and it needs to be addressed on a company-wide basis.

Any executive development strategy employed for this purpose should do the following:

- Build a common understanding of the nature of the opportunity or threat
- Create a sense of urgency and a call to action
- Develop a common language for clear communications and dialogue
- Develop the organization and leadership capabilities needed to successfully address the issue

- Develop specific strategies and action plans for seizing the opportunity or thwarting the threat
- Create the context for required business-unit and business-function planning and strategies

In Chapter Eight we show how Weyerhaeuser's Forest Products Company (FPC) addressed critical business challenges through their Leadership Institute.

Summary

As mentioned at the beginning of this chapter, a comprehensive strategy might deal with several or all five of these high-impact uses of executive development. But how can you know whether all are appropriate in your organization or which ones should take priority? The process described in Chapter Two will clearly, reliably point you in the right direction. If you follow Step One, Research and Analysis, faithfully, you can be certain that your strategy and programs will be directly and tightly linked to your marketplace challenges and your business strategy and objectives. And it will be clear which of the five high-impact uses of executive development should be emphasized.

Next Up:

Chapters Four through Eight each cover one of the five uses of executive development, supported by company case studies. Each case is organized as follows:

- *Introduction:* A review of the high-impact use of executive development and its purpose in a corporation
- *About the Company:* An introduction to the case study company, including its recent history and the situation that prompted the implementation of executive development
- *The Challenge:* The situation that promoted the implementation of executive development, including a list of the desired objectives to be achieved through executive development
- *The Solution:* A detailed account of the prescribed program or system and how it was implemented
- *Results:* A summary of the results achieved

For each case study there is a "Program at a Glance" figure for easy reference to program objectives, details, and results. Table 3.1 presents all the case studies in this format.

Table 3.1. Case Study Composite Programs at a Glance.

	Texas Instruments	UBS	Trinity Technology	First Bank of Sweden	Consolidated Bank	Weyerhaeuser Leadership Institute	Weyerhaeuser Forest Products Co.
Program Title	Creating Our Future (COF) Workshop	UBS Leadership Institute	New Directors Program	The Leadership Forum	Accelerated Leadership Program (ALP)	The Weyerhaeuser Leadership Institute	The FPC Leadership Institute
Participants	Top 250 leaders	Chairman's Office, Group Executive Board (GEB), Group Managing Board (GMB) and the 600 most senior leaders worldwide	Employees entering director-level positions, or new hires at director level	10 high-potential managers	200 high-potential leaders	Top 500 executives	Initially top 200 executives, then top 1,500
Themes	• TI Vision and Strategic Direction (first year) • Innovation and New Business Development (second year)	• Creating and Achieving the Vision and Strategic Agenda	• Linking new director development to business strategy, or "leading from the middle"	• Creating a new Leadership Institute • Accelerating the development of the Bank's best talent	• Managing for Value	• One company, with inspiring leaders aligned around the Roadmap	• The Leadership Challenge • Creating and leading a customer- and market-driven enterprise • Developing our capabilities and creativity • Leading the charge— running a total business

(Continued)

Table 3.1. Continued.

	Texas Instruments	UBS	Trinity Technology	First Bank of Sweden	Consolidated Bank	Weyerhaeuser Leadership Institute	Weyerhaeuser Forest Products Co.
Objectives	• Produce a shared TI view of the future • Test and enhance the vision and strategy and produce the best possible strategy • Improve the strategic skills of senior executives • Understand what it will take to implement the strategy	• Shape UBS's strategic agenda and build unity, alignment, and capacity for execution • Ensure the successful transition of senior leaders into GMB and develop critical leadership benchstrength • Ensure senior leaders have the understanding, knowledge, and capabilities needed to support the strategic agenda	• Understanding Trinity's vision and strategy and the director's responsibility in aligning the organization • Articulating role of director and recognizing the shift in scope and responsibilities from the manager level • Assessing direct staff capabilities of directors and identifying actions to build a high-performing team • Leveraging the role of director and leading from the middle • Adopting renewed	• Expediting the growth, development, and readiness of high-potential candidates • Achieving desired business outcomes • Improving business acumen, perspective, and strategic thinking among participants • Having graduates of The Leadership Forum become exemplars for other leaders to model • Working effectively across boundaries within and outside of the Bank	• Accelerate participants' development • Build a better understanding of the total enterprise • Work across organization on real, current business challenges—create a sense of teamwork • Make leadership talent a competitive advantage • Create excitement about market opportunities • Develop stronger capabilities to achieve business goals and meet customer commitments • Live the corporate values	• Develop critical leadership capabilities to grow the business safely and profitably • Accelerate the "New Weyerhaeuser" cultural change • Orient new leaders from other cultures (acquired companies) to the company's vision, values, and strategies • Create a cadre of diverse leadership talent that will be a source of competitive advantage • Help leaders capture the true business	• Create unity of purpose and commitment to FPC's vision, values, and principles • Build a customer- and market-driven enterprise • Improve leadership skills and instill a sense of responsibility for leading FPC into the future • Develop a broad business perspective and ownership attitudes and competencies • Become more creative and innovative in running the business

	Texas Instruments	UBS	Trinity Technology	First Bank of Sweden	Consolidated Bank	Weyerhaeuser Leadership Institute	Weyerhaeuser Forest Products Co.
			sense of ethical leadership • Helping directors assess their own personal leadership skills against key characteristics of highly effective people • Applying a proven framework for effectively managing a leadership transition			value of a streamlined one-company approach • Develop the capabilities to provide inspiring leadership to employees and create excitement and positive energy in their organizations about the company's future	• Improve communication, cooperation, and a sense of teamwork across unit lines
Content	• User-centered planning module • Analysis of four competitors • Experiential team building • Leadership Challenge, Crafting our	• Annual Strategic Forum • Key talent management mentoring and succession • Senior Leadership Conference • Global Leadership	• Several hours of presession work • Two days on Trinity business context (simulations, strategy discussion, panel) • Two days on Personal Leader	• Presession reading materials (The Leadership Forum Web site, 360-degree feedback process) • Segment One: Action learning (eleven days	• Kickoff session • Presession individual assessment (IDPs, performance coach) • Leadership Challenge (three sessions, action learning) • Closing event	• Segment One: Building alignment around Weyerhaeuser's Roadmap • Taking an external look • Segment Two: Inspired Leaders Inspiring Others	• (See Themes)

(Continued)

Table 3.1. Continued.

	Texas Instruments	UBS	Trinity Technology	First Bank of Sweden	Consolidated Bank	Weyerhaeuser Leadership Institute	Weyerhaeuser Forest Products Co.
	Future presentations	Experience family	Effectiveness (fireside chat, CEO close) • Social networking in evenings	in classroom sessions and about 25% of work time over four months) • Segment Two: Three-month break (one-on-one coaching, selected readings) • Segment Three: Four Demands of Leadership • Segment Four: Leadership Development workshop		• "Intrapreneurship" segment • Five Stages of Innovation • The Four Demands of Leadership • Personal leadership stories • Building Tomorrow's Team	
Length	One week	Varies, depending on content module	Several hours of presession work plus four days in session	One year	6 months, not including optional post-program exercise	Two six-day "weeks" over a three-month period	Four week-long sessions over a twelve-month period
Frequency	Yearly	Ongoing, annual offerings	Four times per year	One cycle per year	Three classes per year	Four or five per year	Eight to ten sessions started each year

	Texas Instruments	UBS	Trinity Technology	First Bank of Sweden	Consolidated Bank	Weyerhaeuser Leadership Institute	Weyerhaeuser Forest Products Co.
Class Size and Mix	Groups of 25 who represented diverse businesses, functions, cultures, and geographies within the company	• Annual Strategic Forum—top 60 • Mentoring—top 200 • Senior Leadership Conference—top 600 • Global Leadership Experiences—approx. 25 to 35 key position holders	15 new directors	10 high-potential managers	Approximately 65 per class	Groups of 25, mix of many different parts of the Weyerhaeuser business	25, including segment for spouses
Faculty	Each session is opened by a Strategy Leadership Team member and closed by senior TI executives	Mostly internal leadership, Group Executive Board, Group Managing Board	Mix of outside faculty and esteemed Trinity executives, including a discussion with Trinity CEO	Internal staff, bank president, external experts and coaches	6 internal and 18 external coaches, external experts, key customers, internal team consultants, executive sponsors	Internal leaders, external experts	CEO, leading university faculty, and consultants, included customers with feedback
Location	Off-site	UBS Corporate Center, various corporate offices	Company facilities	Online, off-site	Off-site	Vancouver B.C. and San Diego, CA	Off-site (three different locations)

CHAPTER FOUR

CREATING STRATEGIC UNITY AND ALIGNMENT

As we noted in Chapter One, a majority of respondents to our most recent survey of trends in executive development identified changes in their business strategy as a top factor influencing their development efforts. That survey reemphasized for us the continuing importance of aligning organizations behind new strategies.

These results, seen in the context of our previous surveys that showed a similar trend, support our belief that creating strategic unity and alignment is one of the five high-impact uses of executive development. We strongly believe that no team, function, business unit, or company can achieve peak performance without a high degree of strategic unity. To reiterate, a high degree of strategic unity exists in an organization when these conditions are in place:

- A compelling vision, inspiring values, and a winning strategy
- Deep understanding, ownership, and commitment throughout the organization
- Aligned goals and actions among business units, teams, and individuals
- The capabilities (mindsets, knowledge, and skills) required to achieve the vision, live the values, and execute the strategies (starting with the company's executives)

In our experience, most organizations do not have strategic unity—and the problem starts with the strategy-formulation process. All too often, a company's vision and strategy are concocted by a small group at the top—typically the CEO and his or her top executives. The vision and strategy they come up with is typically turned over to the company's PR department for the creation and implementation of a comprehensive communication campaign. This can include speeches, newsletters, videotapes, and town-hall meetings. At the end of the day, the troops may know the catch phrases of their management's vision and strategy, but they can't be said to have a deep understanding or to have bought into management's ideas.

At the beginning of a new project we typically perform a needs assessment to identify the executive capabilities necessary to achieve the company's vision and execute its strategies. We usually interview a cross section of executives as part of this process. We always ask them, among other things, to describe their company's vision. With surprising frequency, we get such responses as, "I don't really know," "We have one, but it's not really helpful or useful," or "We have a good vision, but we don't really have a strategy to implement it." Or worse yet, we hear several distinctly different versions of the vision from executives.

It's not much fun to report such findings back to the CEO, who generally reacts with great frustration. On one occasion, after hearing our report of statements like these, an exasperated CEO fumed, "That's just not possible! All I've been talking about for the last three months is our vision and strategy! I've visited every part of our company and spoken to over four thousand employees!" We had to gently remind him not to shoot the messenger.

Traditional methods for communicating strategies for corporate communication tend to employ processes that are passive and mostly one-way. They give the appearance of effectiveness while they are being implemented. But then, a year or so down the road, something happens to make it painfully obvious that a common, clear, and consistent understanding of the vision and strategy does not exist.

So what's a CEO to do?

We believe that an important lesson (with a slight twist) can be taken from Phil Alden Robinson's 1989 film, *Field of Dreams*, starring Kevin Costner. The film's premise was a mystical one. A farmer hears a voice that tells him, "If you build it, they will come." This became the tagline for the film. The farmer interprets it as an order to build a baseball stadium in the middle of his cornfield so that a famous maligned baseball player can return from the past to vindicate his name.

A slightly changed version of this tagline could be adapted for the purposes of strategic unity and alignment: "If they build it, they will come." We believe that to achieve a high degree of strategic unity, a much broader base of executives and other implementers must be intimately involved in the strategy formulation process. People will never truly "get it" unless they are somehow engaged at the visceral level. Active engagement results in a higher-quality strategy and deeper understanding, ownership, and commitment to it. It will also lead to improved strategic thinking, better execution, and better business performance. But, hang on—we're getting ahead of ourselves.

Case Study: Texas Instruments

The Texas Instruments case is a great illustration of building strategic unity through a high level of engagement of large numbers of executives.

About the Company

With 34,900 employees in 25 countries and nearly $10 billion in annual sales, Texas Instruments (TI), located in Dallas, Texas, has found its niche as one of the world's largest semiconductor makers and the market leader in digital signal processors (DSPs). Over half the wireless phones sold worldwide contain TI's DSPs, which are also found in wired communications, digital consumer cameras, and video products.

In the early 1990s, TI—along with such companies as Intel, National Semiconductor, and Cypress Semiconductor—was dubbed one of the "new alchemists who can turn sand into gold." During this period, often referred to as the Golden Age of chips, semiconductor sales growth was expected to exceed 40 percent by 1995. Total industry volume was expected to more than double to $350 billion in 2000.

It was a turbulent time for the industry. In response to these expected heavy demands, chipmakers saturated the market, which led to an oversupply of chips and created a boom-to-bust cycle.

TI CEO Jerry Junkins expressed his conviction that the company had to adjust to the new industry dynamic. Tragically, Junkins suffered a fatal heart attack during the second year of our work with the company. In a *Fortune* magazine article it was reported that as Tom Engibous, Junkins' successor, "accelerated changes that Junkins had set in motion, he transformed TI from a large, unfocused colossus with a reputation for arrogance to a linchpin of the digital communications revolution."

The Challenge

Junkins had believed that TI's other businesses—software, materials and control, calculators, printers, notebook computers and defense electronics—were too "siloed," as were their leaders and leadership development programs. TI senior business leaders—veterans, some of whom had been with the company 25 years or more—would see each other only at annual meetings, which typically focused on the performance of the individual business units. Junkins felt that in many ways TI was just the sum of its parts. He led the company to conclude that TI's future success depended on becoming "one great company" rather than a collection of individual businesses.

Achieving that goal demanded not only that TI create a new vision of the future and a strategy to realize it, but also that it build and forge a very high degree of unity and alignment throughout the worldwide organization.

One of the first steps TI took was to adopt a new team process that resulted in the creation of the new TI Strategy Leadership Team. This team consisted of the office of the chairman, the chief executive, all of TI's business presidents, the CFO, the general counsel, the head of HR, the head of communications, and the senior executive marketing, quality, R&D, and supply teams. The Strategy Leadership Team saw their general purpose as consisting of four major elements:

- Defining and nurturing the strategic direction for TI
- Ensuring quality decisions
- Ensuring that decisions were deployed
- Ensuring the development and placement of leaders throughout the company

The fourth element was especially critical. TI knew it needed change. Its vision for change required a cadre of leaders who understood the resulting strategy and had the knowledge, skill, and abilities to lead consistently with that strategy.

But George Consolver, director of the TI Strategy Process, was concerned about the imminent rollout of a new vision and strategy formulated by the Strategy Leadership Team. He worried that the strategy deployment process that had been used in the past—namely, turning over the vision and strategy to the public relations staff, who would develop a comprehensive internal and external communications strategy—would not work in this case.

We met with Consolver and Hank Hayes, then chairman of TI's Strategy Leadership Team in Dallas. Hayes said, "The truth of the matter is that we've got a substantial gap between where we are today and where we need to go. We've got to start devising ways to meet those goals. It's not going to happen just because we've got a goal. It's going to take some far different behavior on our part."

Hayes also described what he hoped would come from the process: "We want wide participation across the company in helping to shape and build the strategy. . . . We'll then have a rejuvenated strategy for the corporation that we've really thought out."

The challenge was to convince TI's senior executives not to go the traditional deployment route. Rather, we all agreed that we wanted them to take the version of the new vision and strategy they had created and treat it as work in progress, paving the way for engaging those 250 leaders from all over the TI world in a different kind of process.

The combination of Hayes' enthusiastic "let it rip" line of attack and Consolver's more cautious, deliberative approach proved successful. They convinced TI's Strategy Leadership Team to, in effect, put a "Draft" stamp on the current version of the vision and strategy and then begin a unique and innovative approach to creating strategic unity and alignment.

This was no small accomplishment, given the tendency of many CEOs and senior executives to believe that vision and strategy is "their job." This mindset is relinquished only reluctantly by a company's top brass, who find it very threatening to let people below them on the corporate ladder muck around with vision and strategy. The notion is completely counterintuitive because it works against their paradigm that vision and strategy are their responsibility and that, frankly, they know best.

The Solution

It was during our meeting with Consolver and Hayes that the initial idea for the Creating Our Future workshop emerged. This workshop was designed to address several important business objectives:

- Produce a shared TI view of the future
- Test and enhance the vision and strategy and produce the best possible strategy
- Improve the strategic skills of senior executives
- Understand what it would take to implement the strategy

In addition to aligning business units, function teams, and individuals to a strategy and vision, TI placed critical importance on developing the capabilities required to achieve the vision and successfully execute the strategy.

The Creating Our Future workshop ran for one business week (five days); it was conducted off-site and attended by groups of 25 who represented diverse businesses, functions, cultures, and geographies from TI offices all over the world in order to promote optimal teamwork and collaboration. Each session was opened by a Strategy Leadership Team member and closed by one or more senior TI executives (see Exhibit 4.1 for the agenda).

Exhibit 4.1. The Creating Our Future Windowpane Agenda.

Monday	Tuesday	Wednesday	Thursday	Friday
The future marketplace: convergence and competition	User-centered planning	TI strategy presentation The Leadership Challenge	Crafting our future • Implementation challenge • Critical success factors • Barriers/actions	SLT dialogue • Presentation • Reactions
The future marketplace: customer panel	Team learning	TI strategy • Evaluation • Improvements • Opportunities and challenges	Crafting our future • Create presentations • Dry runs • Finalize	SLT open exchange Key insights and celebration Adjourn
Learning lab			Celebration dinner	

The fundamental design concept for the one-week workshop had two major components driving the process. The first component (which took place during the first half of the workshop) replicated as identically as possible the same process of strategic thinking and analysis that the Strategy Leadership Team had gone through to create their initial draft version of TI's vision and strategy. The second component of the workshop actively engaged all of the top 250 leaders, soliciting their suggestions for improving the vision and strategy and asking them to identify critical success factors for implementation. (See Figure 4.1.)

Developing market foresight was a critical aspect of the first half of the Creating Our Future workshop. A set of TI's customers, suppliers, and industry experts participated in the first day of the workshop. Participants explored multiple perspectives on the industry. Customers shared their points of view, weighing in on what it would take to be the industry leader.

TI executives attending the Creating Our Future workshop also gained perspective on the marketplace by listening to the outside industry expert. The expert painted a picture of what global business and competition and the industry would look like in the future and what the key drivers would be.

A unique aspect of this analysis was that it was done side by side with key customers. Think about working with your customers as learning partners! Customers provided their perspective regarding future markets, what these implied for TI, and how they saw TI compared with the future portrait described by industry experts.

One of the most intriguing aspects of the first half of the Creating Our Future workshop was the User-Centered Planning module, which engaged a consultant who uses a cultural anthropologist's approach to understanding customers. Their materials included the results of videos, reviews, and analysis of hours of customers' interaction with TI products.

George Consolver gave us his reflections about this part of the program: "We wanted to gain a perspective on the impact of our products and technologies. The cultural anthropologists taught us how people live, learn, work, and play, and how

Figure 4.1. First and Second Creating Our Future Linkage.

1st COF

- Enhanced strategy & ownership
- Increased market foresight
- Improved teamwork across TI
- Critical success factors identified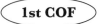

2nd COF

#1 Success Factor:
Innovation & New Business Creation

to think about our technology within those contexts. This was one of the most popular segments of the program—our engineers in attendance actually discovered and started to think about *people,* not just technology!"

This user-centered session was followed by teams conducting an analysis of various likely competitors. In this exercise, the teams played the role of the competition's top management, tasked with creating a five-year winning strategy that included neutralizing TI's business strategy and strengths.

All of these exercises were completed during the first half of the workshop, before participants saw the draft version of the company vision and strategy. The process was designed this way to provide the most comprehensive picture of the strategic forces confronting TI and to achieve buy-in on the seriousness of these challenges.

Midway through the workshop, participants engaged in experiential team building aimed at accomplishing three objectives:

- Develop a sense of the total enterprise and encourage cross-organization collaboration
- Prepare participants to work together on the Leadership Challenge project to enhance TI's strategy
- Provide key leadership skills necessary to take full advantage of each participant's heterogeneous learning team or workshop group

Participants then received the Leadership Challenge, which was to craft and create their own version of the future. Starting with the Strategy Leadership Team draft version of the strategy as a baseline, the subgroups were given their assignment: "Given all that you have heard in the workshop so far, and all that you knew before you arrived, what do you think would make the strategy even better?"

Besides being asked to improve the vision and strategy, the teams had to identify the critical success factors (CSFs) for implementation, including challenges to be addressed and barriers to be overcome. They also identified key actions they would take to begin implementing the strategy in their business units. Their work evolved into draft Crafting Our Future presentations, on which participants got critiques and received peer feedback from each other in dry runs.

In the workshop finale, on day five of the program, participants presented their findings and recommendations (their final Crafting Our Future presentations) to Strategy Leadership Team members for questions and feedback.

Results

A challenge that came up early on was how to capture the best ideas that were coming out of each workshop. TI didn't want nine versions of the vision and strategy—they wanted one. The solution was simple but elegant. A committee was formed by taking one volunteer from each of the nine Creating Our Future workshops. The volunteers' job was to represent their workshop session. The committee was charged with the task of developing a "best of the best" version of TI's vision and strategy. This version was presented to the Strategy Leadership Team, which finalized it and presented it back to the entire set of 250 leaders in an exciting, high-energy leadership conference at the end of the year.

TI believes that Creating Our Future has paid off in many ways. Consolver noted:

- Movement of the company from midindustry to top financial performance rankings, with dramatic stock price and P/E increases
- Improved quality and ownership of the strategy
- Increased unity and alignment around the vision and strategy
- Increased team spirit and excitement about TI's future
- Expanded understanding of the marketplace
- Increased long-term strategic thinking
- Improved collaboration among executives across the business

Consolver saw positive outcomes for all stakeholders touched by the workshops: he described it as a real maturing process for the participants. They gained an expanded understanding of the present and future marketplace, and they increased their long-term strategic capabilities. He also observed that both the quality and the ownership of the strategy improved because of the workshops, and that the end product was much more streamlined than the vision draft. He observed a much greater sense of team spirit and collaboration as well as a sense of excitement about the future.

Even participants whose businesses would decrease in importance in TI's portfolio made such statements as, "I get it; I understand. . . . I don't necessarily like it. But I support it and I can go back to the office and explain it to the people who work for me."

Here are their comments (reprinted with permission from Texas Instruments' internal newsletter). Kerry Miller, TI's manager of communications, who attended one of the early sessions of Creating Our Future:

> I had a unique opportunity a month ago. . . . It was a chance to attend one of the nine TI strategy workshops being conducted this year. These workshops give an in-depth look at the new TI business strategy—in draft form—developed over the past year by the TI Strategy Leadership Team.
>
> It was unique, because for five days I and about 30 other TI people were immersed in every aspect of our company. We talked about our past and our future, our markets and our products, our customers and our suppliers, our competitors and our allies, our strengths and our weaknesses, our hopes and our fears.
>
> And we talked about us—the people of TI. About who we are and what kind of company we want to be a part of. We got into the strategy in detail, even talking to the market consultants who are helping TI analyze the future, and customers who have a vested interest in us.

At the end of it all, we were asked to give our frank opinion of the draft strategy—what makes sense, what doesn't and what suggestions we have for making it different.

Here are some of the things from the week that will stay with me for a long time.

The challenge: In the first hour of the workshop, George Consolver introduced our task as "helping to refine the TI strategy." Bill Mitchell, a TI vice chairman, jumped in and said, "No it's not—your job is to challenge the strategy, not just refine it. We want to know if you believe it, and if you don't, what should change."

Future users: Larry Keeley, president of the world's largest strategic design planning firm, told us TI as a whole isn't focusing enough on the end users of our products: "Great [technology] breakthroughs are ones that gather up the activities of our lives and allow us to handle them in new ways. Human activities are at the core of breakthroughs. Human needs are at the core of those activities."

The creative diversity: [People from TI] in the workshop were divided into four teams. There were six people on my team. Among those six people, three nationalities, four TI business entities and three global regions were represented. Every other team had a similar mix. The combination of minds and backgrounds produced creative solutions to business issues that none of us individually could have produced.

The listening on the last day: Three members of the Strategy Leadership Team—Bill Mitchell, Hank Hayes, and Chuck Nielson—joined us. They listened to our opinions of the draft strategy and the direction it sets for TI. Then they discussed their reactions with us. Their questions stick out in my mind more than anything else:

- Can we be good at everything?
- Can we be in every business?
- How do we get comfortable with choosing a strategy and living with the decisions it drives?
- Could it be that the businesses a corporation chooses to be in aren't as critical to success as the people and strategy processes it uses?

Another outcome that resulted from the nine workshops—one that would prove to be both catalytic and generative—was the identification of the critical success factors required for making the strategy and vision a reality. The number one critical success factor (innovation and new business development) became the theme and focus for the second Creating Our Future workshop. Figure 4.2 shows the areas of focus from the first workshop and their relation to the critical success factor that became a focus in the next workshop.

Creating Our Future became a multiyear architecture for strategy and executive learning.

Figure 4.2. Texas Instruments' Strategy Process.

Following the first year's focus on the TI Vision and Strategic Direction, and the second year's focus on the number-one critical success factor—Innovation and New Business Development—subsequent phases focused on other critical factors for business success, such as reshaping the business portfolio and building business acumen, as shown in Exhibit 4.2.

The Creating Our Future workshops became interwoven with, and integral to, the fabric of TI's existing business planning process and calendar. In effect, TI has fully integrated their strategy and executive development processes.

Summary

The TI case is a dramatic example of how executive development can not only be linked to strategy, but also be part of the process of strategy formulation, in which strategy skills are improved and a high degree of strategic unity and alignment is achieved or created.

Case Study Two: UBS

Our second case provides an excellent example of how a Leadership Institute can be used to communicate top management's strategic agenda, build unity and alignment, and also develop the executive capabilities needed to achieve the agenda.

Exhibit 4.2. Phases of Strategic Actions Following COF.

Phase 1: TI *vision* and *strategy direction*

Phase 2: Achieving our vision through *innovation*: The leader's role

Phase 3: Reshape and focus TI business portfolio

Phase 4: Quality of strategy and *business acumen*

Phase 5: *Talent leadership*

Phase 6: *Customer focus*

Table 4.1. Texas Instruments'
"Creating Our Future" Program at a Glance.

Participants	Top 250 leaders
Themes	• TI Vision and Strategic Direction (first year) • Innovation and New Business Development (second year)
Objectives	• Produce a shared TI view of the future • Test and enhance the vision and strategy and produce the best possible strategy • Improve the strategic skills of senior executives • Understand what it will take to implement the strategy
Content	• User-centered planning module • Analysis of four competitors • Experiential team building • Leadership Challenge, Crafting Our Future presentations
Length	One week
Frequency	Yearly
Class Size and Mix	Groups of 25 who represented diverse businesses, functions, cultures, and geographies within the company
Faculty	Each session is opened by a Strategy Leadership Team member and closed by senior TI executives
Location	Off-site

About the Company

Based in Zurich, Switzerland, and comprising more than 66,000 employees, UBS is the world's largest wealth manager, a premier investment bank, a key global asset manager, and the market leader in Swiss retail and commercial banking. The company began to position itself as a global leader through a series of acquisitions in the 1990s, culminating in the purchase of PaineWebber in 2000. The acquisitions resulted in the formation of four business groups under the UBS umbrella (see Figure 4.3).

As UBS has grown and evolved, so have its challenges and opportunities.

The Challenge

In early 2002—following years of mergers and acquisitions, the expansion of its Group Executive Board (GEB—the top management team) and Group Managing Board (GMB—the top sixty leaders), and the recent appointment of its new president (now CEO), Peter Wuffli, UBS found itself at a critical point in its development. If the firm wanted to succeed, it needed to align its multiple business groups—each with distinctive cultures and business processes supporting different dimensions of financial services—to a consistent, unified strategy.

Although each of UBS's business groups offered best-in-class capabilities to its individual clients, the firm's senior leaders felt UBS was positioned to offer even more value to its clients. As a result, UBS shifted its strategic focus to an integrated business model driven by organic growth. "UBS creates value for its clients by drawing on the combined resources, relationships, and expertise of our individual businesses," CEO

Figure 4.3. UBS Business Group Structure.

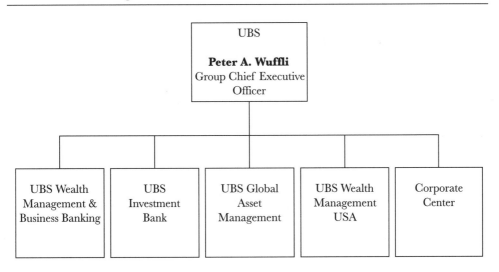

Wuffli said. "This integrated business model is driven by the strength, depth, and alignment of the senior leadership team."

CEO Wuffli believed that the best way to achieve strategic unity and alignment was to define a clear vision and set of values and develop exceptional leadership talents who communicate and embody them.

The Solution

To meet this challenge, the UBS Leadership Institute was launched in 2002. The UBS Leadership Institute was designed to help drive UBS toward a common corporate identity and an integrated leadership team focused on driving organic growth that is closely aligned with the strategic agenda of the firm. Wuffli described the mission: " . . . to develop our most senior leaders through the UBS Leadership Institute as a means to directly align with and in support of our firm's vision, values, culture, and identity and to support them in promoting the critical elements of UBS identity and strengthening the culture required to achieve accelerated and sustained growth throughout UBS."

To achieve this mission, the UBS Leadership Institute would focus on building the leadership capabilities of the firm's senior management team. It would be not a bricks-and-mortar institution but a global team committed to serving its clients: the chairman's office, the Group Executive Board, the Group Managing Board, and the six hundred most senior leaders worldwide.

Under the leadership of Robert Mann, member of the Group Managing Board and global head of learning and development, and in cooperation with the business groups, the UBS Leadership Institute designed the UBS Leadership Development System (see Figure 4.4). These interlinking, complementary programs, processes, and products provided results-focused learning experiences aligned to UBS's vision and values, strategic business needs, industry issues and trends, and practical leadership challenges. Collaboration with leaders across all UBS Business Groups and external organization development experts like Executive Development Associates would ensure that the program design and development process was creative, interactive and dynamic, enriched with knowledge of best practices and continuously integrated feedback.

Creating the Vision. Historically, the Group Managing Board had an annual face-to-face meeting in which the firm's senior leaders gathered to review strategy. Shortly after the Group Executive Board and Group Managing Board were expanded, the UBS Leadership Institute was commissioned to redesign this event to help build alignment among the new leadership team members, dramatically changing the event to a strategic planning session, with networking and relationship building as a key additional benefit of the process.

To build momentum around the firm's new strategic focus, the annual meeting was rebranded as the Annual Strategic Forum, with the first forum themed "Creating Our Future."

Prior to the event, a draft version of the new UBS "Vision & Values" (including Business Goals, Financial Targets, and the Integrated Business Model) was distributed to senior leaders for their feedback.

Figure 4.4. UBS Leadership Development System.

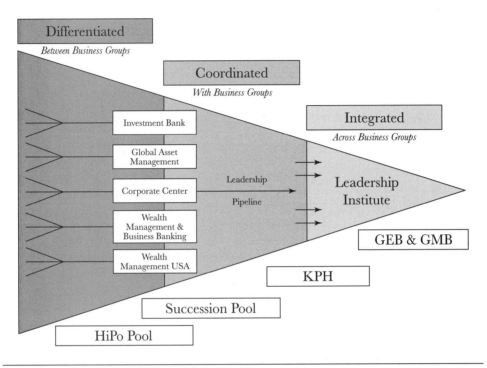

Note: HiPo Pool: High-Potential Talent Pool. *KPH:* Key Position Holders

During the Annual Strategic Forum, participants reviewed their consolidated feedback (over 140 pages of commentary) and discussed and analyzed it in working teams and in plenary sessions.

At the Annual Strategic Forum, the UBS Leadership Institute launched a mentoring program for senior leaders, with Group Executive Board members serving as mentors for the Group Managing Board to further facilitate cross-business communications, alignment, and leadership development. Considered a key component of the alignment strategy, this linking of the top sixty leaders in UBS provided exceptional contributions to leadership benchstrength development, talent mobility, succession planning, business project execution, and ongoing communications among the participants.

By the end of the Annual Strategic Forum, the top sixty senior leaders in the firm produced a new UBS Vision and Values for Action that described behaviors critical for achieving the vision and identified key challenges to achieving this vision.

Communicating the Vision Following the Annual Strategic Forum, UBS's senior leaders understood that to drive the UBS strategy forward, they had a personal responsibility to live the UBS vision and values and communicate them throughout the firm.

To support them, the UBS Leadership Institute team developed the UBS Identity Workshop: Vision & Values, which was delivered by all Group Managing Board members in eight months with UBS Leadership Institute support. Through these workshops, an additional one thousand senior leaders were quickly and personally engaged in the vision and values process. They discussed and identified solutions to the key challenges critical to achieving the UBS strategy. From these workshops, the UBS Leadership Institute team summarized and reported important trends and themes to the firm's senior leadership as well as used them to guide further development of the next generation of UBS Leadership Institute programs.

The UBS Identity Framework—a matrix of characteristics connecting the UBS Vision, Values, and Brand—became a powerful tool to communicate and illustrate the integrated culture senior leaders were striving to cultivate. According to Mann,

"We realized that only when our brand was demonstrated to be consistent and integrated with our vision and values did the combination have the effect we wanted them to have. We define our identity as UBS Identity = Vision + Values + Brand" (see Figure 4.5).

Figure 4.5. UBS Identity Framework: Vision, Values, and Brand.

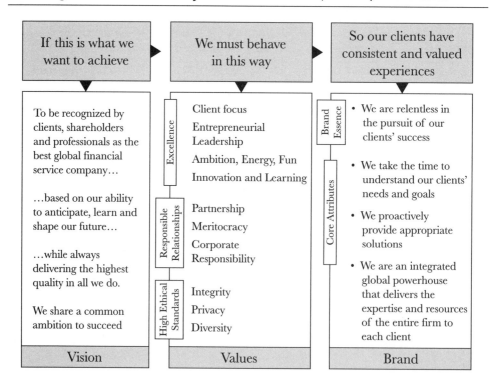

Living the Vision. The momentum generated by the Annual Strategic Forum and UBS Identity Workshops established the UBS Leadership Institute as a critical medium for communicating business strategy and facilitating alignment to it.

Mann and his team created a value proposition (see Exhibit 4.3) for the Leadership Institute to elaborate the specific ways in which they would support the UBS vision: to be recognized as the best global financial services company.

In addition, they realized that the value proposition needed to be supported by an effective value delivery system (see Figure 4.6); that is, the specific processes and programs by which they would consistently deliver the promised Leadership Institute value proposition.

Here are details about the key UBS Leadership Institute programs and processes shown in Figure 4.6:

Annual Strategic Forum. The UBS Leadership Institute was given the mandate to redesign this event, and it was relaunched in 2002 as the Annual Strategic Forum. It is now an annual meeting of the sixty most senior leaders, with a focus on building alignment within that leadership team through strategic planning sessions, with networking and relationship building as benefits of the process.

Mentoring. Another key mandate launched at the Annual Strategic Forum was a mentoring program for senior leaders in which UBS's most senior leaders, the Group Executive Board, mentored the next level of senior leaders, the Group Managing Board. The mentoring program was considered so successful that it was cascaded down to the next level of over two hundred leaders.

Senior Leadership Conference. Following the tremendous success of the redesigned Annual Strategic Forum, the UBS Leadership Institute was asked to redesign and deliver another event: the Senior Leadership Conference, a biennial gathering of the top six hundred global leaders across UBS, traditionally held in Interlaken, Switzerland. The overall objective of the redesigned Senior Leadership Conference was to build unity, alignment, and capacity for execution around the UBS strategic agenda.

The first Senior Leadership Conference in 2003 proved to be groundbreaking in more than one respect. Because the outbreak of SARS and its impact on global travel made it impractical to gather participants in a single conference location, the UBS

Exhibit 4.3. UBS Leadership Institute Value Proposition.

- Facilitating the development of critical strategic and leadership capabilities that reach across all UBS Business Groups

- Ensuring these critical capabilities are embedded in the UBS culture and are continuously refined to a world-class edge

- Providing a common understanding and sharing of best practices to ensure strategic alignment and effective networking among the senior leadership team

- Serving as a strategic catalyst and providing a forum for leaders in UBS to influence critical issues for the firm's growth

Figure 4.6. UBS Leadership Institute Value Delivery System

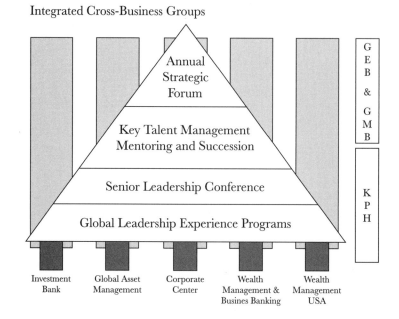

Integrated Cross-Business Groups

Leadership Institute still offered the Senior Leadership Conference, but in a completely new format. Instead of convening in one location, senior managers interacted with their colleagues around the globe via a ninety-minute satellite broadcast and a three-hour local event that took place concurrently in New York, London, Zurich, Tokyo, Singapore, Sydney, and Hong Kong. This first UBS Leadership Institute–designed Senior Leadership Conference was themed "One Firm . . . One Brand . . . One Future" and focused on the launch of a single UBS brand.

The result? "It was so successful," says Mann, "that it was decided to hold the Senior Leadership Conference every year instead of biennially, alternating between a centralized location event and global broadcast via satellite to multiple locations. We've been able to dramatically increase buy-in and the effectiveness of our communication with senior leaders around the world as well as virtually enhance alignment and execution of strategy."

Global Leadership Experience. Since its inception in 1999, more than six hundred senior leaders have participated in a Global Leadership Experience (GLE) executive development program (see Figure 4.7). The GLE programs are highly regarded and enjoy excellent brand recognition throughout UBS. In 2003, the GLE began a new phase when it was expanded to include two additional programs that support the achievement of key aspects of the UBS strategic agenda.

This family of three interlinking executive development programs combines internal and external subject experts with program project work focused on the firm's strategic

Figure 4.7. The Global Leadership Experience Family of Programs.

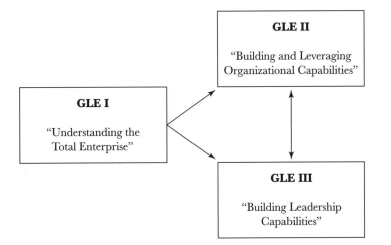

Figure 4.8. UBS Leadership Development Framework.

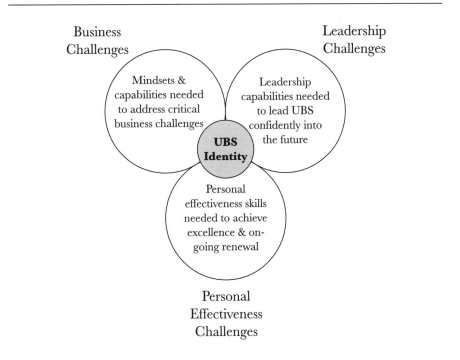

direction. The UBS chairman, CEO, and members of the Group Executive Board and Group Managing Board nominate senior leaders to participate in the program, and they themselves participate regularly as program sponsors, as leaders, and as faculty. Much of the teaching during each Global Leadership Experience is conducted by UBS's most senior leaders, adding business-specific expertise to the sessions and signaling the willingness of UBS's leaders to personally invest in the firm's education processes.

The Global Leadership Experience programs are custom designed to align with the firm's strategic agenda and evolve continuously to reflect strategic challenges, industry best practices, and contemporary learning methods. Faculty and program designs change over time, and new technologies, post-program coaching, and measurement tools are incorporated as appropriate.

The architecture used to design all three Global Leadership Experience programs is based on Executive Development Associates' three-dimensional framework for leadership development, with the UBS identity squarely in the middle.

Global Leadership Experience I: Understanding the Total UBS Enterprise.
The purpose of this Global Leadership Experience program is to develop a deeper understanding of the entire UBS organization and stimulate collaboration among business groups in order to leverage the firm's collective capabilities (see Table 4.2).

Global Leadership Experience II: Building and Leveraging Organizational Capabilities.
This program helps participants delve deeper into the businesses and develop a common view of the current key strategic issues facing UBS (see Table 4.3). They analyze and develop specific organizational actions and measures to enable UBS to strengthen its client focus and integrate capabilities from the whole firm to drive sustained organic growth and foster entrepreneurial leadership behavior.

Global Leadership Experience III: Building Leadership Capabilities.
The purpose of this program is to build the personal leadership capabilities needed to execute the firm's strategic agenda (see Table 4.4). Focusing most closely on the

Table 4.2. Global Leadership Experience I.

Title	Strategic Objectives	Design Principles	GEB and GMB Role
Understanding the Total Enterprise	• Provide overview for all UBS business group products, services, successes, and challenges • Facilitate cross-business integration through networking and identification of integrated business model opportunities	• External faculty presentations • Internal UBS business leader presentations • Case studies • Simulations • Leadership challenge course	• Open and close program • Deliver presentations about their business groups: challenges, opportunities, and successes

Table 4.3. Global Leadership Experience II.

Title	Strategic Objectives	Design Principles	GEB and GMB Role
Building Organizational Capabilities	• Teach participants to articulate their value propositions so that they can construct a more client-focused value delivery system • Teach participants to become entrepreneurial leaders to support organic growth	• External faculty presentations • UBS business leaders serve as facilitators • Group work • Success story presentations	• Open and close program • Present business case for entrepreneurial leadership and organic growth at UBS • Discuss examples of entrepreneurial leadership and organic growth at UBS

Table 4.4. Global Leadership Experience III.

Title	Strategic Objectives	Design Principles	GEB and GMB Role
Building Leadership Capabilities	• Challenge participants to examine their leadership behaviors and effectiveness and create a plan for resolving a critical business challenge • Focused on business challenge	• 360-degree feedback • UBS business leaders serve as teachers • Action learning • External executive coaches • Peer coaching teams • Post-program: mini survey • Coaching • Technology-supported • Follow-up activities	• Open and close program • Teach the four UBS leadership capabilities on which the course is built • Share personal leadership stories • Present business case for leadership development

Table 4.5. UBS Leadership Institute Program at a Glance.

Participants	Chairman's office, Group Executive Board (GEB), Group Managing Board (GMB), and the 600 most senior leaders worldwide
Themes	• Creating the Vision • Communicating the Vision • Living the Vision
Objectives	• Shape UBS's strategic agenda and build unity, alignment, and capacity for execution • Ensure the successful transition of senior leaders into GMB and develop critical leadership benchstrength • Ensure senior leaders have the understanding, knowledge, and capabilities needed to support the strategic agenda
Content	• Annual Strategic Forum • Key talent management mentoring and succession • Senior Leadership Conference • Global Leadership Experience family
Length	Varies, depending on content module
Frequency	Ongoing, annual offerings
Class Size and Mix	• Annual Strategic Forum—top 60 • Mentoring—top 200 • Senior Leadership Conference—top 600 • Global Leadership Experiences—approximately 25 to 35 key position holders
Faculty	Mostly internal leadership, Group Executive Board, Group Managing Board
Location	UBS Corporate Center, various corporate offices

"Personal Effectiveness" dimension of the three-dimensional framework, participants apply leadership concepts, tools, and techniques to specific business challenges, seeking sustainable performance results.

Results

The UBS Leadership Institute is an excellent example of how a leadership development function can rapidly position itself to become not only a force in developing senior leaders but also a key driver of an organization's strategy. UBS has already made tremendous progress toward achieving its vision, and the UBS Leadership Institute is committed to fulfilling its value proposition, creating new processes that facilitate the alignment and development of senior leaders and cross-business teamwork in support of its integrated business model. (See Table 4.5 for the UBS Leadership Institute Program at a glance.)

The UBS Leadership Institute now reports directly to the CEO. According to Mann, "With our vision and values being communicated effectively and senior leaders fully subscribed to the UBS vision, UBS is positioned well for success. The UBS Leadership Institute is determined to sustain stakeholders' commitment and maintain alignment to ensure that UBS does indeed become recognized as the best global financial services company."

Summary

The UBS case is a remarkable example of an executive development function that moved itself from a position of primarily reacting and responding to tactical demands for support toward being a critical means for achieving the firm's strategic agenda—including, most importantly, building a high degree of unity and alignment around business strategy and the strategic agenda.

Next Up:

Chapter Five deals with the perplexing challenge of helping managers who have just been newly appointed into the executive ranks to make that difficult transition successfully.

ENSURING THE SUCCESSFUL TRANSITION OF NEW EXECUTIVES

Each major transition in a manager's career brings significantly different responsibilities, requiring new capabilities (mindsets, knowledge, and skills) for success. In many companies, these transition points include, at a minimum:

- The first time managing other people
- The first time managing managers
- The first executive-level position

Failure rates are high when managers step into these new roles without effective preparation and support. According to Edward Betof, author of *Just Promoted!* and senior vice-president of Manchester Partners International, "Within eighteen months of assuming a new position, four of ten managers and executives receive poor performance appraisals, resign, or get fired." This statistic was based on a survey of more then one thousand managers and executives and their bosses. Betof notes that interview subjects cited six key reasons for failure during the first eighteen months on the job:

- Newly hired or promoted managers and executives were confused about what their bosses expected of them
- Subjects were unable or unwilling to make tough business decisions
- The learning curve was too steep—it took too long for managers and executives to learn the elements of their jobs

- They failed to build successful team relationships and partnerships with subordinates and peers
- Internal politics tripped them up—they lacked the savvy required to understand the political underpinnings of their organization
- They could not effectively balance their professional and personal lives

When someone moves into the executive ranks, this sort of failure must be avoided—"trial and error" as a learning method is just too slow, painful, and costly for the individual executive and the organization.

In our experience, development strategies and programs aimed at helping with these critical transitions must do the following:

- Clarify the person's role and responsibilities as an executive
- Ensure that participants have the capabilities required to perform successfully to meet both the general needs of executives in transition as well as the particular needs of the individual involved in the new job
- Minimize management error and failure rates
- Ensure leaders' understanding of their role in achieving the organization's vision, living its values, and executing its strategy
- Convey understanding about how the organization works cross-functionally and how to best leverage cross-functional capabilities to get things done in the organization and in the marketplace
- Provide networking with other executives, establishing strong working relationships

Such efforts demonstrate a company's commitment to the development, support, recruitment, and retention of new executives.

Case Study Three: Trinity Technologies

This case is an excellent example of an effective executive development solution to the challenge of ensuring that newly appointed executives make a successful transition.

About the Company

One organization that hasn't fallen into the trap described by Betof is Trinity Technologies (not the company's real name, as the staff we were working with at the time have since left the organization). Trinity is a leading computer hardware manufacturer. During the dot-com era its hardware solutions for hosting Web sites were determined to be some of the best in the industry. Its reputation was further enhanced by its development of tools for software designers.

When the new economy evened out, leaving many of Trinity's customers in its wake, the company lost a good portion of its lead and had to diversify its portfolio of offerings—and alter its way of thinking—to retain its prominence. On a business strategy level, Trinity transformed itself. It evolved from a "box" to a "solutions" company. Products became more interactive or "integratable" with other systems. Innovation was still important, but so was execution. Teams needed to know not just how their product worked but also how it fit into a much larger framework for their clients.

Trinity has responded with a number of adjustments, including manufacturing lower-end servers that can run on multiple platforms, exploring high-end data centers, and expanding its client base to include the government.

The Challenge

Trinity has supported executive education through its overarching structure, Trinity University, comprising a core curriculum for training, including support for transitioning leaders as well as development for the company's most senior leaders. One of the fundamental courses at Trinity University is its New Directors program. At Trinity the transition from manager to director is a big deal; director is the first rank of the executive level—the top 2 percent of company personnel.

Trinity had a two-part, two-phase program for new directors in place, but attendance wasn't mandatory. The course, which included general topics such as marketing, was interesting and thought-provoking, but it didn't align enough to the business needs.

A vice president of international sales felt the current pool of directors in his territory lacked the caliber, capabilities, and development opportunities necessary to effectively lead in their market. He wanted a more formal development program that specifically addressed Trinity's business strategy.

The executive development team followed up by helping to create a new level of education for Trinity executives in Europe—one that was much more comprehensive than those they'd had in the past. It was, as a team member describes it, a "mini-'MBA' program with a strategy component."

With this more customized and effective version of programming as a model, Trinity invited us to assist with the process of transforming the curriculum of the existing New Directors Program in the United States.

Linking New Director Development to Business Strategy. Trinity's CEO wanted to make sure the "new" New Directors Program recognized the potential power of the participants to motivate employees while translating the Trinity strategy and what it means to them and the organization. He was keenly aware that newly appointed directors can really be powerful in terms of effecting change—he refers to them as the "switching fabric," where connections and execution happen. At Trinity, this is also called *leading from the middle.*

The development team had learned in an employee survey that a significant portion of Trinity's employees didn't understand the company strategy. New directors, in particular, were uncertain about what sort of effect they would have on it.

Trinity and our EDA program designers determined that a large function of the director role was to understand how horizontal linkages in the company—working cross-functionally—were crucial to achieving business strategy.

The New Directors Program that already existed needed to be refined to align with Trinity's new emphasis on horizontal linkages (that is, working across functions).

In their 2000 book, *The Leadership Pipeline*, Ram Charam, Steve Drotter, and Jim Noel identify a set of critical transitions that individuals go through during their careers in organizations. "Turn 1" indicates the transition from individual contributor to a manager of others—that is, a shift from just managing oneself to managing others. Charam, Drotter, and Noel believe that this transition, like all other major role transitions, brings with it a requirement for new skills and work values. Those new skill requirements include

- Planning work
- Filling jobs
- Assigning work
- Motivating others
- Coaching and measuring others' work

Key work values for this transition include

- The value of getting things done through the efforts of others
- Actually valuing management rather than just tolerating it
- Viewing other people's success as critical to one's own

Transition (turn) 2 is defined as a shift from managing others (typically other individual contributors) to managing and leading other leaders.

Key skill requirements for this transition include

- Selecting and training first-line managers
- Holding first-line managers accountable for managerial work
- Measuring their progress as managers
- Deploying and redeploying resources among units
- Managing the boundaries that separate units that report directly (as well as other parts of the business)

Critical work values for this transition include

- Valuing a pure management role
- Thinking beyond one's own function and concerning oneself with strategic issues that support the overall business
- Valuing the role of leader as coach

Transition 3 signifies movement from the role of manager or leader of leaders to the role of business leader. This is the transition that is most relevant to the new director at Trinity.

This transition demands skills that include

- Communicating through layers of management (vertically) and likely horizontally (for example, geographically) among dispersed direct reports and peers
- Managing areas outside one's own expertise (and being able to understand and value others' expertise in these areas)
- Being able to play as part of a team with other functional and business managers
- Networking
- Competing for resources based on overall business needs and strategic thinking

Important work values include

- Increased managerial maturity around thinking and acting like a businessperson with the right mindset
- The need to have a "total business" view
- A broad and long-term perspective
- The ability to consider futuristic, state-of-the-art possibilities
- The ability to take into consideration the needs of other functions besides your own

The Solution

The first step in the process of redesigning the New Directors Program was to be sure to link executive development with business strategy; therefore we needed to review Trinity's vision, strategy, and business challenges and then determine the organizational and leadership capabilities required by directors to carry them out.

Executive Development Associates and the Trinity development team set out to identify these capabilities. We started by surveying all Trinity vice presidents companywide, then interviewing ten key vice presidents with global responsibility. Some of these leaders were part of a preexisting group at Trinity comprising recognized leaders: the Executive Council, a group of senior and high-potential leaders who acted as an advisory board for executive and leadership development. The interviews covered Trinity's marketplace challenges, vision, and strategy, and the organizational and leadership capabilities required to meet them.

The resulting data provided the foundation for the curriculum to support Trinity's strategy and culture change; that is, the basis for the *new* New Directors Program (see Figure 5.1).

The Program Design. The new program was called Taking Charge: Success Strategies for New Directors. No longer did new directors in Trinity's cosmos get a half-hearted request to attend; it was now a mandatory requirement. All new directors had

Figure 5.1. Core and Foundation Needs from Interviews.

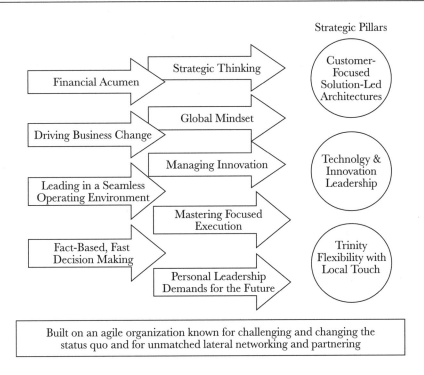

to enroll in the program within the first three to six months after being hired or appointed to a director-level position.

The objectives of the program included

- Understanding Trinity's vision and strategy and the director's responsibility in aligning the organization
- Articulating the role of a Trinity director and recognizing the significant shift in scope and responsibilities from the manager level
- Assessing direct staff capabilities of directors and identifying actions to build a high-performing team
- Leveraging the role of director and leading from the middle
- Adopting the renewed sense of ethical leadership that's demanded in a complex business world
- Helping directors assess their own personal leadership skills against highly effective people who display the best characteristics of leadership and personal mastery
- Applying a proven framework for effectively managing a leadership transition

For the first program cycle, a memo was sent to all Trinity vice presidents and directors from the executive vice president of human resources, announcing the new program. The EVP asked senior management to allow new directors to take off the time necessary to complete the course. The EVP also personally sent out invitations to all those who would be participating.

Having the support of Trinity's senior leadership was critical for creating momentum. It generated a level of excitement around the program, making it seem more a privilege than an obligation.

New Directors Program Logistics. About fifteen new directors participated in the first session; four more sessions were planned for the following year. An online information center was provided; there participants were invited to register for classes, review schedules and logistics, make arrangements for travel and accommodations, and read up on relevant subjects in an online library.

To orient new directors before taking the New Directors course, several hours of preliminary work was required online, including the following:

- Interviewing two vice presidents or veteran directors to gain insight into transitioning into the director role
- Clarifying and discussing expectations about the new director's role with the participant's manager and one key staff member
- Completing advance reading materials, specifically Harvard Business School professor Michael Watkins' article on transition challenges and Trinity's vision and strategy statement
- Completing the self-guided application on Harvard Interactive's Web site on transitions (specifically, Watkins's modules on diagnosing the situation, building the team, and aligning with the boss)
- Completing a survey identifying participants' transition issues and challenges
- Reviewing case studies
- Identifying and beginning analysis of a specific leadership dilemma they faced in their own transition—that is, a difficult situation they faced or a choice they had to make that they felt was critical to the business or their personal success

The presession work also introduced participants to the Eight Core Tasks of an Effective Transition.[1]

- Diagnose the situation you face
- Assess your vulnerabilities and avoid common traps
- Accelerate your learning and the transition process

---

1. Adapted from Watkins's "Core Transition Tasks" in *The First 90 Days,* Harvard Business School Press, 2003.

- Prioritize and plan for early wins and long-term successes
- Build a productive relationship with your boss
- Assess and develop a strong team
- Create supportive internal and external partnerships
- Align strategy, structure, processes, skills, and group culture

Figure 5.2 describes the New Directors Program design.

Table 5.1 presents the four-day program agenda, which has two parts—focusing on business and organizational issues the first two days and on personal leadership skills and concepts the last two days.

The evenings are dedicated to social and networking activities to encourage relationship-building among participants.

Having Trinity's senior leadership involved in the program is crucial to making it a success. The development team balanced the content of the New Directors Program

Figure 5.2. The New Directors Program Design.

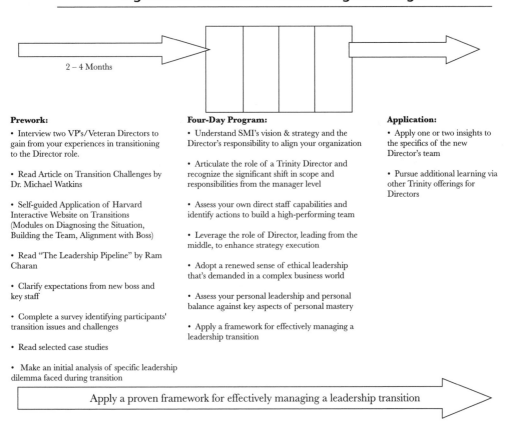

2 – 4 Months

Prework:

• Interview two VP's/Veteran Directors to gain from your experiences in transitioning to the Director role.

• Read Article on Transition Challenges by Dr. Michael Watkins

• Self-guided Application of Harvard Interactive Website on Transitions (Modules on Diagnosing the Situation, Building the Team, Alignment with Boss)

• Read "The Leadership Pipeline" by Ram Charan

• Clarify expectations from new boss and key staff

• Complete a survey identifying participants' transition issues and challenges

• Read selected case studies

• Make an initial analysis of specific leadership dilemma faced during transition

Four-Day Program:

• Understand SMI's vision & strategy and the Director's responsibility to align your organization

• Articulate the role of a Trinity Director and recognize the significant shift in scope and responsibilities from the manager level

• Assess your own direct staff capabilities and identify actions to build a high-performing team

• Leverage the role of Director, leading from the middle, to enhance strategy execution

• Adopt a renewed sense of ethical leadership that's demanded in a complex business world

• Assess your personal leadership and personal balance against key aspects of personal mastery

• Apply a framework for effectively managing a leadership transition

Application:

• Apply one or two insights to the specifics of the new Director's team

• Pursue additional learning via other Trinity offerings for Directors

Apply a proven framework for effectively managing a leadership transition

Table 5.1. New Directors Program Windowpane Agenda.

Trinity Context: Business and Organizational		Personal Leadership Effectiveness	
Day One	Day Two	Day Three	Day Four
8:30 – 10:30 A.M. Introductions and road map for the program Simulation emphasizing: • Understanding the role of the director (leading from the middle) • Leading horizontally	8:30 A.M. – 12:30 P.M. Execution: Leading from the middle • Assessing and building your team (based on assessment information) • Leading through influence – networking and coalitions	8:30 A.M. – 12:30 P.M. • Leadership: What's it all about? • Development edge: Derailment factors and strategies to avoid vulnerabilities	8:30 A.M. – 12:00 P.M. • Leading through values: What do I stand for? • Alignment: What relationships need tending? • My legacy • Message map
10:30 A.M. – 12:30 P.M. Defining the director role; debrief VP; interview insights; group develops first-pass role definition	• Managing up for alignment and to secure resources • Balancing strategic and tactical decisions and priorities		
Lunch			

1:30 – 3:30 P.M.
• Vision and strategy (Sr. VP)
• Dialogue: What does this mean to us? Adaptive challenges? Impact on director role?
	1:30 – 3:00 P.M.
	• Panel: Lessons learned; how-to's on leading from the middle
	• Assessing personal vulnerabilities in the director role
		1:30 – 5:30 P.M.
		• STAR Model: Building the organizational architecture
		  • Diagnosis
		  • Hot topic groups
		• What is your value add?
		• Subordinate expectations (Bennis model)
			1:00 – 3:00 P.M.
			• Executive Group: Reflection and challenge
			• Participants present director role and highlights of "What do we need from the top to be successful?"
			• Have CEO close the session

3:30 – 5:30 P.M. • Translating strategy into my unit; how my unit fits; my vision and role of my organization • (Create and share message maps)	3:15 – 5:30 P.M. Ethical leadership dilemmas: Business leadership without easy answers		

| Trinity Context: Business and Organizational | | Personal Leadership Effectiveness | |
Day One	Day Two	Day Three	Day Four
Dinner			
7:30 – 8:30 P.M. • Create presentation: "How We Now See the Role of Director" (to present later in week) • Homework: My team assessment	7:30 – 9:30 P.M. • Social activity: Targeted to build and nurture networking and new relationships	7:30 – 9:00 P.M. • Leading through personal values	

with a mix of outside faculty and Trinity senior executives, including a discussion with Trinity's CEO on leadership and Trinity's values. These discussions are saved for the end because looking forward to this portion of the program is a strong motivator for the participants and helps ensure that they remain engaged throughout. The nature of the discussion—informal and intimate—was in keeping with Trinity's open dialogue philosophy. Participants are encouraged to ask questions and pose challenges. The feedback on these sessions has been enormously positive; they remain in the program today.

Trinity's CEO still makes regular appearances, as do other senior executives, whose "fireside chats" have become a highlight of the program.

Results

Trinity's development team is starting to measure the impact of Taking Charge. Most of the recorded impact has come via participant feedback.

Participants found the new emphasis on aligning the program with strategy to be extremely beneficial. "I liked the fact that this course didn't dance around the real issues at [Trinity]," wrote one of the new directors.

Another of the Trinity executives who completed the course commented on the greater clarity it brought to his role: "This program brings fresh, new perspectives to my job, and the specific timing is great. The entire class was very relevant and the difference between manager and director became much more apparent. I am now much more clear about what I need to do to be effective."

In a feedback survey, participants rated the program at an average of 4.74 (*highly effective*) on a five-point scale.

A certain momentum has evolved around this program. When the Trinity University team contacts new directors to solicit their participation, people listen and are excited. Supervisors readily make the necessary time allowances for the directors reporting to them. Now, in terms of involvement, people are engaged, motivated, and challenged.

Summary

In Trinity Technologies we see an effective process for ensuring that newly appointed executives succeed, reducing costly errors and turnover (see Table 5.2 for the program at a glance).

Next Up:

Chapter Six deals with the crucial process of building benchstrength rapidly by accelerating the development of an organization's pool of emerging leaders.

Table 5.2. Trinity New Directors Program at a Glance.

Participants	Employees entering director-level positions, or new hires at director level
Themes	Linking new director development to business strategy, or "leading from the middle"
Objectives	• Understanding Trinity's vision and strategy and the director's responsibility in aligning the organization • Articulating the role of the director and recognizing the shift in scope and responsibilities from the manager level • Assessing direct staff capabilities of directors and identifying actions to build a high-performing team • Leveraging the role of director and leading from the middle • Adopting a renewed sense of ethical leadership • Helping directors assess their own personal leadership skills against key characteristics of highly effective people • Applying a proven framework for effectively managing a leadership transition
Content	• Several hours of presession work • Two days on Trinity business context (simulations, strategy discussion, panel) • Two days on Personal Leader Effectiveness (fireside chat, CEO close) • Social networking in evenings
Length	Several hours of presession work, plus four days in session
Frequency	Four times per year
Class Size and Mix	Fifteen new directors
Faculty	Mix of outside faculty and esteemed Trinity executives, including a discussion with Trinity CEO
Location	Company facilities

CHAPTER SIX

ACCELERATING THE DEVELOPMENT OF EMERGING LEADERS

The breadth, depth, and rate of change in organizations, environments, jobs, and positions makes it essential that a company's emerging leaders are developed in the most effective and expeditious way. It is imperative that the most important capabilities (mindsets, knowledge, and skills) needed by an organization's emerging leaders are known and fully "baked into" their preparation for future higher levels of leadership responsibility. This is crucial both for continuous individual executive development and for organizational performance and effectiveness. It seems very clear now that the irreversible shift to the Information Age, the growing need and intensifying demand for first-rate executive talent, and the trend toward job- and company-hopping will feed this benchstrength challenge for many years to come.

The growing need for top-notch executive talent is very much a function of the increasing complexity of the content and context of many executive jobs, roles, and positions.

The University of Michigan Business School's Executive Education periodic survey of the most pressing problems confronting managers and organizations also attests to the need for more high-caliber managerial talent. Here are their recent results for the top ten pressing problems:

1. Attracting, keeping, and developing good people
2. Maintaining a high-performance climate
3. Thinking and planning strategically

4. Managing time and stress
5. Producing high-quality goods and services
6. Staying ahead of the competition
7. Improving customer satisfaction
8. Aligning vision, strategy, and behavior
9. Maintaining work and life balance
10. Improving internal processes

Clearly, resolving these top ten problems will require ever more competent, flexible, and learning-agile executives.

Given the focus of this chapter on accelerating emerging leaders, it's important to highlight what the University of Michigan's survey identified as the number one problem confronting managers and organizations: attracting, keeping, and developing good people!

EDA's current research on trends in executive development (see Chapter One) confirms the University of Michigan survey: the need to increase benchstrength is the number-one factor influencing today's corporate executive development efforts, and it is also predicted to be the number-one objective for executive development strategies and programs over the next few years.

The number-two objective in EDA's survey was accelerating the development of high potentials. In this chapter, we present innovative approaches for using executive development to increase benchstrength through the acceleration of high-potential talent in two major corporations.

Case Study Four: The First Bank of Sweden

The First Bank of Sweden case study is an example of how implementing an executive development program designed for a new leadership institute also became a means of preparing and retaining high-potential talent.

About the Company

The First Bank of Sweden, located in Stockholm (confidentiality requires us to refrain from identifying the bank here, so First Bank of Sweden is a pseudonym) is a relatively small organization with fewer than 1,500 employees. Owned by the government of its home country, the Bank is an organization with an unusual mission and charter—namely, "To make a unique and significant contribution to the success of dynamic and innovative entrepreneurship in Sweden."

First Bank of Sweden provides both a unique executive development challenge and an unusual organizational setting. In most organizations, when attempting to ground your executive development planning within the larger environmental context, it is often a bit of a leap of faith to connect to its impact on the national interest. Not so with First Bank of Sweden. Given that its charter is to support entrepreneurship in its home country, one of the many ways that First Bank of Sweden has worked on fulfilling its mission has been to aid start-ups and support them with consulting services required for survival and success.

First Bank of Sweden serves exclusively small and medium businesses with its lending and is increasingly oriented to growth in the knowledge-based sectors. The Bank is part of its country's broader strategy for identifying and capitalizing on opportunities to improve productivity and innovation in the economy.

The Bank emphasizes a philosophy of strategic partnering. When it develops new products or activities, it develops them in niches that are typically underserved in the market. One example is the seed funds created by the Bank. Its rationale for these funds is twofold: first, to fill a critical gap that exists in the marketplace; second, to take advantage of the opportunity to create the funds in partnership with other institutions.

Enacting this networking philosophy is but one example of the kinds of challenges that First Bank of Sweden confronted in the pursuit of its mission.

The Challenge

In 2002, the Bank administered an employee engagement survey (soliciting opinions and attitudes) and got some extremely disappointing feedback about the lack of leadership development opportunities available in the organization. Around that same time, the Bank also became aware of a lack of readiness of people in the talent pool for the most senior executive team level positions. In a sense, this served as a double wake-up call—an alarming set of survey results and the sudden awareness of a critical lack of benchstrength—that got the Bank's senior leadership team to agree to put these items on the agenda of an upcoming meeting.

We got a chance to help when one of us was invited to the meeting to talk about leadership development best practices and what the Bank might do to address their double-barreled challenge.

During that meeting with the Bank's senior management team, the CEO was quite taken with the parts of the presentation we made related to mentoring and to creating an "institute" dedicated to leadership development. As part of our presentation—which included best and innovative executive development practices at leading companies—the CEO heard about how Roger Enrico, CEO of PepsiCo, held off-site retreats at his personal ranch with a small group of high-potential senior leaders.

This meeting catalyzed a series of other meetings and discussions at First Bank of Sweden. The concept of the program we discuss in this chapter arose to address simultaneously the building of benchstrength for senior-level positions and the general gap in leadership development opportunities identified in the employee engagement survey. The notion was to move forward with a single initiative—one that would address these needs and also take advantage of the CEO's interest in mentoring.

The Solution

We saw an opportunity to address both issues in one solution: identify the best high-potentials at First Bank of Sweden and provide them with an action learning project that would provide development opportunities throughout the Bank.

The Leadership Forum. The Leadership Forum was the initiative created by First Bank of Sweden. The core idea for The Leadership Forum was to identify ten high-potential managers at the Bank—those who could potentially be candidates to fill senior executive positions on the top management team (that is, direct reports to the CEO). The Leadership Forum would provide an accelerated leadership development process for those high-potential managers and simultaneously address the other challenge—increasing leadership development opportunities in the Bank—by having the high-potential managers work on an action learning project to create a new leadership institute.

More specifically, The Leadership Forum had the following objectives:

- Accelerate the development of high-potential managers in order to build bench-strength—that is, to increase the quality and quantity of replacements for senior leadership positions
- Use participants as an action learning team to recommend objectives, architecture, components, and success measures for a world-class leadership institute
- Develop visible improvements in leadership capability
- Strengthen business acumen, broaden perspectives, and improve strategic thinking skills
- Help participants become role-model learners and leaders
- Build strong working relationships to enhance working across organizational boundaries

The first objective clearly addresses the challenge of managing individual talent: to expedite the growth, development, and readiness of their best high-potential candidates. The second objective relates to addressing the employee engagement survey feedback about the lack of leadership development opportunities at the Bank. Objectives three and four focus on the observable and tangible improvements in participants' leadership skills that the program was seeking, especially those related to business acumen, perspective, and strategic thinking. The fifth objective reflects the Bank's interest in having graduates of The Leadership Forum become exemplars for other leaders to model—leaders growing and teaching other leaders. The final objective addresses another potential leadership capability that First Bank of Sweden believed was critical—working effectively across boundaries in and outside the Bank.

Design for The Leadership Forum. The total program for the ten handpicked high-potential executives spanned a one-year period (see Figure 6.1).

Figure 6.1. The Leadership Forum.

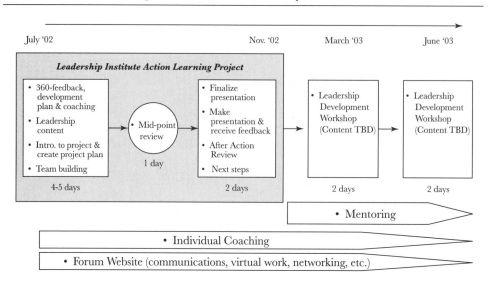

The first major phase—the first four months—of the program was an action learning project. During those four months the executives spent eleven days in classroom sessions and about 25 percent of their normal work time in their action learning project teams, working on the creation of the Leadership Institute.

The Leadership Forum had a very special and unique action learning project, personally sponsored by the president of First Bank of Sweden. Participants were charged with recommending the objectives and design of a new Leadership Institute that would provide the leadership development opportunities so badly needed in the Bank. To that end, they were to answer the following questions:

- What recommendations do you have to support the creation of a First Bank of Sweden Leadership Institute that will aim to significantly strengthen First Bank of Sweden's quality of leadership and leadership development efforts and to enhance its position as an employer of choice?
- Given our mandate, marketplace challenges, and strategies, what are the common, priority development needs at each key level of management in First Bank of Sweden?
- What did we learn from benchmarking organizations recognized for their best practices and achievements in this area that will help us to capitalize on this opportunity? (The action learning project required participants to benchmark other leading companies' leadership institutes.)
- What should be the mandate and objectives of the Leadership Institute?
- What should be the architecture of the Leadership Institute?

- What structures, systems, and processes will be required to support the Institute in delivering its mandate?
- What should be the governance model for the Institute? How will the Institute make decisions on priorities, strategies, and resources?
- What should be the key components of the Institute?
- Which current leadership development strategies, systems, and programs should be enhanced?
- What new leadership development systems, programs, and processes should be incorporated within the Institute?
- How can we best address both the common development needs at each level of management in First Bank of Sweden as well as individual development needs?
- How do we ensure compatibility and synergy of these components under the umbrella of the Institute?
- How should we measure success for the Institute?
- What metrics will we use to monitor progress? To measure success?
- What needs to be done to ensure the Institute remains relevant to the needs of the organization?
- What is the recommended strategy, and what are the recommended priorities, for getting the Leadership Institute launched?
- What are our priorities, given our current and emerging business and leadership challenges?
- What resources are needed?
- How do we enroll and engage senior leadership and the organization as a whole in the creation and operation of the Institute? How do we involve other key stakeholders?

Answering these questions might have given pause to even the most experienced executive development consulting firm or university executive education group. Within the scope of their role in working on this challenge, the ten participants operated very much in the mode of consultants doing high-level, systemic design and development work.

Our role in this phase of The Leadership Forum represented a major shift for our firm as well. Typically acting as experts who diagnose, custom design, and implement executive and leadership development strategies, systems, and programs—the "doers," if you will—we found ourselves in the role of "coach of the doers," that is, coaching the ten participants on the processes and methods (see Chapter Two) to carry out their charter.

Before the participants even convened for Segment One of the action learning phase of The Leadership Forum, they were very actively engaged in critical preliminary work and preparation.

As we mentioned in our footnote definition of action learning in Chapter One, a critical element is the establishment of clear individual and team development goals. At First Bank of Sweden, the critical first step in individual development called for participants to engage in an on-line 360-degree feedback process, using the Bank's existing leadership profile to begin the process of identifying their development goals.

Participants also each had a conversation with their manager in order to complete the learning contract for their participation in The Leadership Forum (covering, for example, their commitments, responsibilities, and expectations).

Presession reading materials before the first five-day classroom session included the book *High Flyers* by Morgan McCall, "War for Talent" research reports by McKinsey Consulting, and our article "The Business Impact of Corporate Executive Development." In addition to doing the reading, assigned teams of two individuals had to prepare a "flash presentation" on what they had read—a fifteen-minute presentation to the rest of the class during the first class session. These dyads were responsible for teaching the larger group the highlights of what they had learned. This was in keeping with the theme of participants taking responsibility for their own learning.

Participants were also required to register themselves on the Leadership Forum Web site, which supported their individual preparation as well as their activities as a team before, during, and after each learning segment. During The Leadership Forum, all the preliminary work and preparation required for each session was done online through the Web site. This included doing the required reading, completing assessment instruments, preparing for presession meetings with managers, and preparing the flash presentations with a fellow participant before the first class session. The Web site also provided the means for the action learning teams to work virtually on their projects in between the classroom sessions.

Segment One of the Action Learning Phase. The first full day of the program focused on both individual and group development and effectiveness. Participants engaged in intensive team building aimed at enhancing their effectiveness on the action learning project as well as building esprit de corps. They also received individual feedback from the results of the 360-degree feedback process they engaged in before the start of Segment One. Participants then scheduled their first one-on-one coaching sessions with the program facilitator—who was also an executive coach—and were exposed to the development planning and follow-through tool (Fort Hill's Friday5s) that would support their growth and development throughout the entire Leadership Forum.[1]

On the second full day of the program, participants began with reflections on the preceding day—an opportunity to capture and discuss key insights from the previous day. This was a process, structure, and habit that would become part of the participants' repertoire of skills. Reflection is a critical part of learning and development, but it is typically seen as a luxury for most busy executives. Reflections were an integral part of all classroom segments of the program.

Participants made their flash presentations to the larger group over the course of several days during the session; they were exposed to trends and best practices in leadership development by Executive Development Associates and other industry experts—grist for their mill in building the First Bank of Sweden Leadership Institute.

---

1. Fort Hill's Friday5s is a Web-based tool that helps users keep course follow-through and goals a priority and track progress over time.

They also reviewed First Bank of Sweden's current leadership development system and initiatives, and they conducted a team analysis of the results of the needs assessment survey we had conducted for them prior to Segment One.

On the evening of the second day, participants were immersed in benchmarking tools and best practices. On the third day of the program, they took a field trip to a leadership development best-practice company to obtain ideas for their new institute and to practice benchmarking. On day four, participants took part in a guest panel process on the lessons of experience and leadership development with chief learning officers from several leading companies. They also created their action learning project plan and did a dry run—a practice presentation to the faculty and the other experts present—of their project plan presentation to get ideas for improvements.

On the fifth day, participants finalized their presentations and made them to their sponsor—the president, the head of human resources, and the chief operating officer. They got feedback and then revised their project plans. Participants concluded the day by using the Friday5s tool, then we previewed what would happen at their midpoint review (the next classroom event).

Action Learning Project Midpoint Review. In between Segment One and the midpoint review, participants used Friday5s to track their individual development goals with the help of their coach, team peers, and manager. They had a one-on-one session with their coach as well a conversation with their manager covering the results of the first segment, a review of the learning contract, and their progress on their Friday5s action plans.

Perhaps most important, they completed work on their action learning project plan, including interviews with senior management team members, board members, and clients about the Bank's leadership development needs. They also conducted several more benchmarking visits to best-practice companies and summarized their findings and reports.

On the first day of the midpoint review, they reviewed and revised their project plan. Later that first day, they began to prepare the presentations of their progress reviews for their sponsors. The morning of the second day, participants reviewed their preliminary ideas and progress with the sponsors and revised their project plans based on their feedback. Their reviews included progress on their leadership development goals. We then previewed Segment Two, the final classroom component of the action learning phase.

Segment Two of the Action Learning Phase. During the two months between the end of the midpoint review and Segment Two, participants worked intensively on their action learning projects. They consolidated all their research results, completed preliminary work on the Leadership Institute recommendations, and consulted with key stakeholders for validation. They also continued implementation of their personal development plans.

The first day of Segment Two began with a review of the team's progress on their development goals, as well as an evaluation of each individual's development progress.

All action learning project work was consolidated, and the final report was prepared: the team's findings and recommendations for the creation of the Leadership Institute, including a suggested implementation plan. The end of the first day was dedicated to finalizing and testing the presentation with faculty.

The second of the two days commenced with the presentation to sponsors and key stakeholders, followed by a dialogue with them. Following this, while the project sponsors deliberated and prepared their response to the final report, the participants conducted an after-action review: What was learned? How could we have done better? How can we leverage what we learned going forward individually and for the Bank? The morning ended with feedback from sponsors and their responses to participants. The afternoon included the planning of next steps.

The action learning team proposed the creation of a governing Leadership Council to oversee and direct the activities, objectives, and operations of the Leadership Institute, as well as the creation of a permanent position with the title of Director, Leadership Institute, reporting to the Leadership Council. The team also recommended the development and implementation of transition management programs that focused on the key transitions between managing self and managing others, and between managing others and leading leaders. The Leadership Forum participants also recommended the continuation of an accelerated development experience for high-potential managers similar to theirs (The Leadership Forum), including an action learning project, personal leadership development, and mentoring by a member of the senior management team.

In addition, the team recommended the establishment of an annual senior management conference to include The Leadership Forum members and the top two hundred bank executives, with annual themes to be chosen by the Leadership Council. Agendas for these conferences would be strategic in nature, and the resulting learning process would be cascaded through the organization by the participants. The team made additional recommendations about critical supporting systems that needed to be addressed, including compensation, performance management, talent management, and executive involvement.

Phase Two of The Leadership Forum. With their action learning project complete, the participants had a three-month break back on the job before convening for the next classroom session, Segment Three.

In the interim, participants had another one-on-one coaching session. They also completed selected readings, prepared a case study on leadership, and prepared for personal leadership storytelling.

The objectives of Segment Three included

- Enhancing individual leadership effectiveness by understanding what the Four Demands of Leadership are, sharing our best practices, and experiencing each demand
- Recommending enhancements to the First Bank of Sweden leadership profile
- Reviewing progress on individual development plans
- Selecting the topic for Segment Four

Segment Three ran for two and a half days. The first full day commenced with the definition of and framework for the Four Demands of Leadership:

- Setting and communicating direction
- Creating alignment among key constituencies
- Setting and living the values
- Growing and developing self and others

The four demands framework is based on the work of Professor Morgan McCall at the University of Southern California, whose research identified the common requirements, or "demands," that all successful leaders must master.

The participants engaged in an interactive case on each of the four demands and identified and shared their own personal best practices for each demand. On the evening of the first day, participants shared personal leadership stories about the events and people who have shaped their beliefs and values, and consequently shaped them as leaders. On the second half of day two, participants engaged in an outdoor, high events challenge course focusing on trust, stretch goals, communication, and teamwork. They then had the chance to debrief their experience in the challenge course using the four demands framework. In effect, the challenge course provided a leadership lab in which they had the opportunity to practice the four demands and provide feedback on their effectiveness to each other.

During the last half-day segment, participants reviewed their progress on their individual development plans and planned Segment Four's leadership development workshop. This was a unique opportunity for participants to once again take responsibility for their own learning and design their own final development segment for The Leadership Forum.

Segment Four of The Leadership Forum. Before Segment Four commenced, participants had another one-on-one coaching session and continued work on their individual development plans. Their presession reading for Segment Four included the book *The Power of Purpose* by Richard J. Leider, who was a part of the faculty for Segment Four. This two-day segment, designed with the input of participants in The Leadership Forum, was focused on more personal aspects of leadership and addressed topics such as these:

- Greater purpose
- Leading from within
- Courage
- Vision and legacy

Results

Several critical outcomes suggested to the Bank that The Leadership Forum was extremely successful.

1. Participants' reactions. A recent internal First Bank of Sweden publication, discussing the work of The Leadership Forum, quoted several participants speaking about their experience with the program:

"Getting the perspective of peers from other parts of the country, benchmarking our organization against world leaders and building a better understanding of our shareholder's expectations has helped me become a better leader. I believe that this is the best investment any organization can make in its people."

"This was the most interesting and mind-expanding activity that I have participated in since I joined the Bank. The hands-on approach of our Senior Management Team, combined with action learning methods, allowed the group to effectively solve problems while gaining a depth of knowledge of First Bank of Sweden's operating environment."

"The Forum has provided a wonderful environment for self-development. It's been a great experience to be brought outside our comfort zone to learn 'new things' and take a look at 'old things' from a new angle."

2. The First Bank of Sweden Leadership Institute is being implemented and continues to thrive.

3. The Leadership Forum was chartered for a second iteration. For their action learning project, the second cohort focused on what can be done to improve the effectiveness of the Bank in supporting the growth of companies in its home country and the leadership of its entrepreneurs. After the second Leadership Forum cohort made their presentation to the CEO and senior vice presidents in attendance, three of their recommendations were endorsed on the spot.

4. Of the twenty participants in The Leadership Forum's first and second sessions, seven have been promoted.

5. Participants also observed that their team was effective because it took ownership of this complex project and delivered on all of its timelines; it had continuous, ongoing, and thorough communication; decision-making was collaborative; and there was universal mutual trust and respect.

Summary

The First Bank of Sweden case is unusual in that a tremendous development investment was focused on their ten "best" high-potential managers, those most likely to fill positions in the senior team. (See Table 6.1 for the First Bank of Sweden's Leadership Forum at a glance.)

Case Study Five: Consolidated Bank— The Accelerated Leadership Program

Our next case study, that of Consolidated Bank, illustrates a massive effort to accelerate the development of nearly two hundred emerging leaders in a short twelve months.

Table 6.1. The First Bank of Sweden's Leadership Forum at a Glance.

Participants	Ten high-potential managers
Themes	• Creating a new Leadership Institute • Accelerating the development of the Bank's best talent
Objectives	• Expediting the growth, development, and readiness of high-potential candidates • Achieving desired business outcomes • Improved business acumen, perspective, and strategic thinking among participants • Having graduates of The Leadership Forum become exemplars for other leaders to model • Working effectively across boundaries within and outside of the Bank
Content	• Presession reading materials (The Leadership Forum Web site, 360-degree feedback process) • Segment One: Action learning (eleven days in classroom sessions and about 25% of work time over four months) • Segment Two: Three-month break (one-on-one coaching, selected readings) • Segment Three: Four Demands of Leadership • Segment Four: Leadership Development workshop
Length	One year
Frequency	One cycle per year
Class Size and Mix	Ten high-potential managers
Faculty	Internal staff, bank president, external experts and coaches
Location	Online, off-site

About the Company

Founded in 1784, Consolidated Bank (a pseudonym) is one of the oldest U.S. commercial banks. With assets over $70 billion and more than thirty thousand employees, its major lines of business included retail/consumer, corporate, and international banking.

The Challenge

We got the opportunity to work with Consolidated Bank when a senior manager for human resources development attended one of our Strategic Executive Development Workshops (SEDW).[2] She had recently received a very exciting directive from the CEO of the bank and sought our advice and guidance during the SEDW session. She explained that Consolidated Bank had recently completed an acquisition; a subsequent employee survey clearly indicated that that there were leadership challenges related to the acquisition and integration of the acquired bank into the much larger Consolidated Bank. The survey indicated that at both banks management needed significant improvement in order to effectively compete in regional and global markets. The CEO wanted a tangible way to build leadership development into the bank's strategy— "Managing for Value"—and to demonstrate that the employee survey feedback was being taken seriously. He also wanted to accelerate the development of identified high-potential leaders in the organization. The goal was to strengthen the ability of these leaders to improve employee satisfaction, promote desired leadership practices, and help achieve the bank's performance goals as well. Developing cross-functional and cross-business-unit perspectives was also recognized as critical to understanding and leading in a new and more complex organization.

The CEO was also very clear about wanting a learning experience that was different and innovative—not the "same old same old." He thought that Consolidated Bank's existing development programs and processes were failing to effect radical change, and he knew that the organization needed to invest in helping its Executive Management Group—made up of himself and the team reporting directly to him— build a world-class organization to meet the needs of their stakeholders. The next generation of leaders needed to be well prepared for expanded future roles in order to achieve their business objectives.

Several cultural imperatives also had to be met, including

- Increased employee involvement, more delegation, and more teamwork
- A commitment to exceeding the expectations of customers
- Embodying leadership practices that included working as a team, encouraging and rewarding initiative, demonstrating uncompromising integrity, recognizing and celebrating diversity, and having fun

The Solution

To address those issues, the executive development team created the objectives of a new program, shown in Exhibit 6.1, which was soon named the Accelerated Leadership Program.

2. SEDW is a three-and-a-half-day workshop in which participants learn how to create high-impact executive development systems and programs linked to their business strategy. Content typically includes actual cases presented by senior executive development leaders from major corporations, benchmarking against research on best practices, executive coaching, action learning, a mini-action learning project to create a custom-designed executive development strategy and program based on a real needs assessment, and the like. SEDW is for both people with less than five years' experience in executive development and more experienced people who need a broad refresher.

Exhibit 6.1. Objectives of the Accelerated Leadership Program.

- Accelerate participants' development
- Build a better understanding of the total enterprise
- Work across organization on real, current business challenges—create a sense of teamwork
- Make leadership talent a competitive advantage
- Create excitement about marketplace opportunities
- Develop stronger capabilities to achieve business goals, meet customer commitments
- Live the corporate values

Design of the Accelerated Leadership Program. A senior-level advisory committee was formed, consisting of leaders from human resources, line executives from various business units, and the Executive Management Group. The advisory committee reviewed Consolidated Bank's business direction and needs, employee survey results, and analyses of performance ratings to help identify and clarify the bank's leadership development needs. Then the advisory committee identified a set of criteria for selecting the Accelerated Leadership Program participants, which included

- High performance and high potential
- Visibility, influence, and number of direct reports
- Congruence with values and practices
- Diversity

The advisory committee identified two hundred leaders and divided them into three groups, or classes, of approximately sixty-five each. All three classes of sixty-five participants were to complete the Accelerated Leadership Program within a year. Figure 6.2 shows the architecture template for the Accelerated Leadership Program, designed to take place over the course of a six-month period following the kickoff session and assessment phases of the program.

Accelerated Leadership Program Kickoff. All two hundred participants were joined by their managers and coaches (we'll have more to say about coaches later) for this session launching the Accelerated Leadership Program. One of the ideas behind the kickoff was to get participants excited about this innovative program. More specifically, four goals were set for the event:

- To create a sense of commitment to the Accelerated Leadership Program among participants
- To show senior management's support of the program
- To provide orientation for the participants to the Accelerated Leadership Program objectives and process and to set clear expectations

Figure 6.2. Accelerated Leadership Program Architecture.

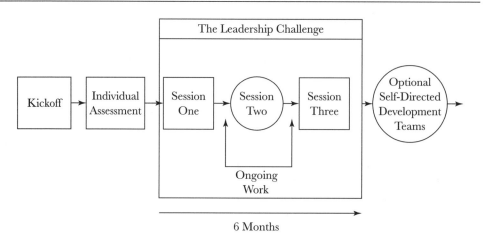

• To celebrate and recognize the accomplishment of being nominated and selected to participate the program

   Speakers at the kickoff included Consolidated Bank's CEO, the president, and the executive vice president of human resources.

Presession Individual Assessment. Before the beginning of Session One of the Accelerated Leadership Program, each participant completed an individual development plan that was based on three assessment tools. Exhibit 6.2 outlines the assessment tools and the individual development planning employed.

   The Consolidated Bank Management Assessment Form, an annual assessment process already instituted at the bank, consisted of feedback from direct reports and managers about each participant's management and leadership strengths and areas for development. The *Managing Personal Growth* (MPG) process defined each participant's job responsibilities, skills needed for success on the job, and personal capabil-

Exhibit 6.2. Consolidated Bank Assessment Process.

• Assessment tools
  • BankBoston management assessment form
  • Managing personal growth
  • Career architect
• Individual development plans
  • 2/1: Two skills to develop, one to leverage
  • Three-way contracting
  • Ongoing coaching and development

ities, comparing these with his or her manager's perception of job priorities and skills and identifying specific actions to enhance the participant's capabilities. *Career Architect®*, a multipurpose tool for planning and managing the development of senior managers, was used to examine core competencies, characteristics, and behaviors of successful leaders and to identify strengths and overused skills.[3]

Each participant completed an Individual Development Plan (IDP). In those plans the 2/1 strategy was used: it included two development needs that had been identified, with action plans for how they would be addressed or improved, plus one strength and how it would be leveraged for even better leadership performance. The program also utilized a three-way contracting process: the individual participant, his or her manager, and the "performance coach" met to agree on and develop a "contract" for the three goals and the action plans for the IDP and set times to review progress on the action plans.

Coaching. The performance coach had these main functions:

- Facilitating the assessment phase by collecting and analyzing assessment data
- Helping to structure participants' IDPs and facilitating discussions with participants and their managers
- Supporting participants' application of learning and coaching them on specific management issues that arose on the job
- Helping participants measure progress against goals

The selection and deployment of coaches was a unique aspect of the program, and, in many ways, far ahead of its time, as coaching was still in its infancy then. At many companies, having a coach meant you were in trouble. Not at Consolidated Bank. Here the best talent were working with coaches to become even better.

All twenty-four coaches (eighteen external and six internal) were chosen through a rigorous vetting process that included extensive interviews. All coaches participated in an orientation and training around coaching within the Consolidated Bank context, and all agreed to work within the three-way contracting process, to be responsible for monthly updates, and to network and collaborate extensively with participants and their bosses during the course of the program. External coaches were contracted to work a set number of hours per participant.

They used a behavioral interview process to decide the dimensions needed in coaches. They advertised in local professional networks and media, received over one hundred responses, and chose the coaches after using the vetting process.

The performance coaching process was a critical component of the Accelerated Leadership Program; one individual on the Consolidated Bank team was tasked with managing the coaching process full-time. She conducted interviews matching coach and participant, scheduled trainings for the coaches, completed monthly progress reports, managed coaching invoicing, and conducted quarterly progress review meetings.

3. *Career Architect* is a product of Lominger Ltd.

In addition to the services provided by the twenty-four performance coaches, it was expected that participants' managers would also serve as coaches on a day-to-day basis.

Session One. Figure 6.3 provides a visual representation of the design of the Leadership Challenge, the main curriculum of the Accelerated Leadership Program. Session One of the Leadership Challenge, which was four and a half days long, aimed to create a shared understanding of global business and strategy and the financial services industry and marketplace, help participants better understand changing customer needs, and build skills to enhance their performance as individual leaders and as leaders of high-performance teams (such as enhancing coaching skills to develop exceptional performance). External faculty shared their expertise, and key customers from every bank segment participated as learning partners by sharing their perspectives and their opinions about Consolidated Bank, bringing firsthand, highly stimulating insights into the session. Additional faculty developed participants' leadership skills.

Business Challenges (Action Learning Projects). Action learning was built into the program to achieve the desired program blend of leadership development and strong business focus. Action learning puts participants together in teams to work on real, current, and pressing business challenges, with the goal of improving the business and developing the participants simultaneously. Accelerated Leadership Program action learning teams were formed during Session One so that participants could apply what they were learning to business challenges that they would work on over the course of the six-month program.

The business challenges that participants worked on were solicited from the Executive Management Group, who created a list of potential projects (challenges) for the

Figure 6.3. Consolidated Bank Accelerated Leadership Program: The Leadership Challenge.

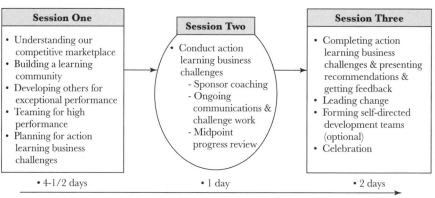

participants to choose from. The challenges were intended to improve the business, facilitate team learning, provide cross-functional exposure, and stimulate innovation.

Exhibit 6.3 illustrates some of the challenges that the Action Learning Teams took on during the program.

Each class of approximately sixty-five participants was divided into eight teams made up of participants from as many different parts of the bank as possible. During Session One project teams were formed, and they selected a challenge. Then they learned and applied business planning, tools, and techniques to create a project plan. They presented their draft project plans to the other teams, the faculty and a real venture capitalist to get feedback and ideas for improving their plans. That feedback proved to be invaluable in modifying their plans at the end of Session One. Significant enhancements in the quality of the plans were the order of the day.

Session Two. Session Two, a one-day session scheduled midway through the Leadership Challenge, provided an opportunity for participants to focus on progress they had made in their action learning business challenges, their learning as a team, and their IDPs. The action learning teams presented the results of their work to date, with preliminary recommendations, and they received feedback from the project sponsors. The midpoint review also provided an opportunity to reinvigorate passion and commitment and to reconnect with sponsors. Perhaps most important, this check-in provided a way of controlling "scope creep" (projects growing beyond their original charter) and making midcourse corrections if projects were not meeting sponsors' expectations. Each team was assigned a team consultant from the Executive Development staff to assist with group dynamics, time management, and final presentations throughout the months leading up to the third session.

Session Three. Session Three provided a forum for the action learning teams to finalize and present their recommendations. On day one of this two-day event, teams reflected on their experience (individual leadership learnings and team learnings),

Exhibit 6.3. Examples of Business Challenges.

- Business-Specific
  - Financial measurement tools for managers
  - Product development process for corporate bank
  - Super market banking opportunities in Latin America
- Customer Focus
  - Drivers of loyalty
  - Customer listening methods
  - Delivery of customer information to front-line staff
- People Practices
  - Improvement of employment function
  - Becoming a Top 10 employer
  - Establishing mentoring programs

synthesized all of their project work, created their final presentations, and conducted dry-run presentations, obtaining feedback and coaching on how to fine-tune their presentations. On day two they made their final presentations to the Executive Management Group, their managers, and their sponsors. They received reactions and feedback, then met one last time to finalize next steps to take their recommendations forward, after the conclusion of the Accelerated Leadership Program. The Executive Management Group and sponsors held meetings to evaluate and decide what action to take on each of the action learning team projects and to reach a final decision: "implement now," "implement next year," or "nice idea, but not implement." Each team received a letter after the program outlining the Executive Management Group's decision and rationale.

As an unexpected result of Session Three, many of the action learning team members found themselves on the speaking circuit, fielding numerous requests for presentations from business unit presidents and Executive Management Group members.

Closing Event. The program ended with a celebration based on the theme of a continuing Leadership Journey, highlighted with a video retrospective. Participants heard presentations from the CEO, the COO, the executive vice president of human resources, and the senior manager for human resources. There was an acknowledgement of each participant's successful completion of the Accelerated Leadership Program in a graduation ceremony and closing reception.

Results

We can look to a variety of sources and perspectives to help in the evaluation of the success and impact of Consolidated Bank's Accelerated Leadership Program. We highlighted the commitment and celebration that accompanied both the start and finish of the program. This was not just a façade; all of the stakeholders were very interested in and excited about this program—and the celebrations were an important symbol of that.

Program evaluations and focus-group results from the participants, their staff and managers, and the performance coaches indicated that the assessment phase, the performance coaching, and the business challenges were some of the high points in the program.

In terms of specific skill and competency improvements, Exhibit 6.4 shows the top four results.

Exhibit 6.4. Top Four Skill Improvements.

• Build valuable networks with people across the organization	92%
• Be a better coach to my staff	84%
• Create an environment that enables team to produce results	65%
• Motivate and develop my staff	62%

Looking back at the objectives of the Accelerated Leadership Program, the improvement in building networks clearly addressed the objectives of enhancing a cross-business-unit perspective at Consolidated Bank as well as developing stronger capabilities to achieve business goals and meet customer commitments—stronger networks made it easier to know whom to go to for what, when, and how, when trying to present a seamless face to the customer.

Exhibit 6.5 details some of the other outcomes that were attributed to the Accelerated Leadership Program.

The senior manager for human resources reflected on why she thought the program was a success.

> Senior Leadership was able to see the key talent of the bank in action and that led to several of the participants receiving key new assignments—something that probably would not have happened prior to Accelerated Leadership Program. Action learning teams continued to meet long after the program ended, and in some cases formed alumni groups.

> Participants came to understand that in order to be effective they had to build relationships across the organization—that was a big deal and a big insight for them. All of the teams were diverse—for an organization that was siloed into lenders, retail bankers, etc.—the program helped to break those silos down and that was critical.

In many ways, the Accelerated Leadership Program was innovative. It had many leading-edge learning processes, such as in-depth multiple assessments, executive coaching (only recently emerging in some large companies), and action learning baked into the design. Not only were these innovative activities ahead of their time, they were also integrated in a very effective way. (See Table 6.2 for the Consolidated Bank Accelerated Leadership Program at a glance.)

Summary

We believe that both the First Bank of Sweden and Consolidated Bank cases serve as rich examples of creative ways of building benchstrength by accelerating the development of high-potential talent. In the First Bank of Sweden case a primary

Exhibit 6.5. Outcomes of the Accelerated Leadership Program.

- Some recommendations were incorporated into reengineering initiative
- Several recommendations were implemented—especially in banking operations areas
- Many participants received significant promotions; some changed career directions
- Few participants left organization
- Cited as one of CEO's proudest accomplishments that year

Table 6.2. Consolidated Bank Accelerated Leadership Program at a Glance.

Participants	Two hundred high-potential leaders
Theme	Managing for Value
Objectives	• Accelerate participants' development • Build a better understanding of the total enterprise • Work across the organization on real, current business challenges—create a sense of teamwork • Make leadership talent a competitive advantage • Create excitement about market opportunities • Develop stronger capabilities to achieve business goals and meet customer commitments • Live the corporate values
Content	• Kickoff session • Presession individual assessment (IDPs, performance coach) • Leadership Challenge (three sessions, action learning) • Closing event
Length	Six months, not including optional post-program exercise
Frequency	Three classes per year
Class Size and Mix	Approximately sixty-five per class
Faculty	Six internal and eighteen external coaches, external experts, key customers, internal team consultants, and executive sponsors
Location	Off-site

emphasis was on preparing next-in-line leaders for top management positions in a way that simultaneously addressed the Bank's overall lack of development opportunities for the general population of leaders. In the case of Consolidated Bank, the primary focus was on expediting the readiness of key talent to take on the increasingly complex marketplace by preparing them for the expanded roles and responsibilities the future would require.

Next Up:

Chapter Seven illustrates how companies can use executive development to meet one of their most daunting challenges: organizational transformation.

CHAPTER SEVEN

TRANSFORMING ORGANIZATIONS

E very company requires a major transformation at some point in its organizational lifecycle. These transformations can be driven by major external challenges, such as hostile takeovers, competitive threats, or mergers and acquisitions. Or conscious choices within a corporation can drive a major organizational change proactively—such choices may go by names such as *reengineering, total quality, turnaround,* and so on.

Executive development forums are a powerful way to support both types of organizational transformation, serving as a catalyst for the required changes and building the organizational and executive capabilities needed to transform.

Organizational transformation is by definition extremely challenging and difficult. Kotter, in his *Harvard Business Review* article "Leading Change: Why Transformation Efforts Fail" (1995), identifies eight pitfalls that contribute to the failure of organizational transformation:

1. Not establishing a great enough sense of urgency
2. Not creating a powerful enough guiding coalition
3. Lacking a vision
4. Undercommunicating the vision by a factor of ten
5. Not removing obstacles to the new vision
6. Not systematically planning for and creating short-term wins
7. Declaring victory too soon
8. Not anchoring changes in the corporation's culture

We have found that many, if not most, of these pitfalls can be addressed and avoided by using custom-designed executive development as a primary means of achieving a corporate transformation. Using Weyerhaeuser as a case study, this chapter will show how one such effort is working its magic.

Case Study: Weyerhaeuser

We begin with a discussion of the factors confronting Weyerhaeuser, then show how the company is using executive development as the major lever in facilitating and accelerating their transformation.

About the Company

Founded in 1900, Seattle-based Weyerhaeuser is in its second century of existence. It is a company with a global orientation and over sixty thousand employees in five hundred different locations. Weyerhaeuser is one of North America's largest producers of forest products, including logs, building products, wood chips, pulp, paper, and packaging. Weyerhaeuser is also a leading recycler of office wastepaper, newspaper, and corrugated boxes. And Weyerhaeuser is one of the leading homebuilders in the United States. The company has been part of the Fortune 200 since 1956.

In 1995, Steve Rogel was named president and CEO of Willamette Industries, a much smaller but very aggressive, fast-moving, successful, and profitable competitor of Weyerhaeuser. He had essentially grown up at Willamette, having started his career there in 1972. In 1997, Rogel was invited by the former president, CEO, and chairman of Weyerhaeuser, Jack Creighton, to take the reins at Weyerhaeuser.

Rogel accepted the invitation to what he described as the biggest professional challenge of his entire career. Within the first few years after the start of his tenure, Rogel and Weyerhaeuser acquired approximately one company every year, including strong industry players like MacMillan Bloedel and Trus Joist. Then came the big surprise! Weyerhaeuser made an unsolicited purchase offer for Rogel's previous employer, Willamette Industries, and Willamette eventually accepted Weyerhaeuser's final bid.

As evidenced by the acquisitions, the early years of Rogel's tenure were a period of intense industry consolidation. Horace Parker, corporate director of strategic education, referred to this period as a time to "buy or be bought."

With the acquisition of McMillan Bloedel, Trus Joist, and later Willamette Industries, the employee population of Weyerhaeuser nearly doubled, from approximately 37,000 to almost 65,000 over the course of about thirty-six months. Parker described the resulting company as a "multicultural polyglot."

The Challenge

There was a pressing need to integrate the diverse cultures and people into Weyerhaeuser to achieve the all-important synergy that determines whether or not acquisitions provide the promised value that drove them in the first place.

Rogel saw Weyerhaeuser's situation at the time as requiring a complete transformation—from the multicultural polyglot into which it had grown to a unified company with an aligned culture, which he had called "one company." And yet he was experiencing many of the challenges and impediments to successful transformation that Kotter identified in the above-referenced article. Unifying and aligning the multiple companies and cultures in Weyerhaeuser was a big challenge.

The Solution

We were invited to assist Weyerhaeuser in exploring how executive development might play a role in this transformation. CEO Rogel asked Parker to head up the project. A senior-level committee of high-potential leaders was chartered to serve as an advisory and oversight committee for the effort on behalf of Rogel and the senior management team.

The first step was to identify the critical development needs—the capabilities (mindsets, knowledge, and skills) needed to successfully transform Weyerhaeuser. We conducted a Web-based needs assessment using our rapid-cycle process (described in Appendix H) that made it possible to quickly obtain input from over one hundred Weyerhaeuser executives (approximately 25 percent of the target audience). A few one-on-one interviews were also conducted with key stakeholders such as business unit vice presidents and the executive committee.

At this time, Parker and his team decided to name the executive development effort the Weyerhaeuser Leadership Institute (WLI). The advisory committee heartily endorsed the name and concept.

The findings of the needs analysis were presented to the advisory committee and then to Rogel and the senior management team. They developed the following overall objectives for WLI:

- Develop critical leadership capabilities to grow the business safely and profitably using appropriate Roadmap tools (*Roadmap* refers to Weyerhaeuser's ten core processes that CEO Rogel wanted used consistently throughout the company—for example, the strategic planning process, purchasing process, value propositions, individual development planning, asset allocation, and so on)
- Accelerate the "New Weyerhaeuser" cultural change to speed, simplicity, and decisiveness
- Orient new leaders from other cultures (acquired companies) to the company's vision, values, and strategies, and learn from these leaders
- Create a cadre of diverse leadership talent that will be a source of competitive advantage
- Help leaders capture the true business value of a streamlined one-company approach (*one company* again refers to the CEO team's desire for the business units to act as a single enterprise and leverage their total capabilities fully in the marketplace, rather than acting as independent fiefdoms as they had tended to do in the past)

- Develop the capabilities to provide inspiring leadership to employees and create excitement and positive energy in their organizations about the company's future

The principal theme of WLI was creating one company, with inspiring leaders aligned around the Roadmap.

Weyerhaeuser Leadership Institute Design. Figure 7.1 shows the high-level architecture for the WLI.

The WLI participants are the top five hundred executives, who attend in groups of twenty-five, in two six-day sessions (Segments One and Two in Figure 7.1) over a three-month period. The groups of twenty-five are a mix from as many different parts of the Weyerhaeuser business as possible. From a transformational perspective, the notion was to start with a critical mass of the most senior leaders and then allow the messages to cascade down into the lower reaches of the organization.

Segment One emphasizes building alignment around Weyerhaeuser's Roadmap. The Roadmap includes Weyerhaeuser's ten core processes that Rogel wanted to be used consistently throughout the company. This alignment-building is a two-step process. Participants first engage in Segment One themselves, and then they teach the material within their own organization. Segment Two aims to inspire participants and develop their leadership capabilities so that they, in turn, can inspire and motivate their own workforce. Weyerhaeuser also created a customized 360-degree leadership feedback instrument based on the specific leadership practices needed to implement the Roadmap.

Figure 7.1. The Weyerhaeuser Leadership Institute

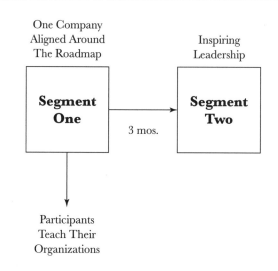

Segment (Week) One: One Company Aligned Around the Roadmap. The objectives for Segment One of WLI include

- Clarifying and discussing Weyerhaeuser's vision, values, and strategies
- Understanding key forces and trends in global business and strategy, and the implications for Weyerhaeuser and its leaders
- Identifying strengths and areas for improvement based on the Weyerhaeuser Roadmap Leadership 360-degree feedback instrument results and creating personal action plans
- Developing a deeper understanding and ownership of the Roadmap and mastering the leaders' role in using the Roadmap effectively

The centerpiece of this first weeklong segment is a custom-designed business simulation to practice running a company using the Weyerhaeuser Roadmap. To provide both content and context before engaging in this simulation, participants have the opportunity to take an external look at the environment within which their company is functioning by hearing from an expert on their industry and global business. They are also encouraged to take an introspective look at themselves—as individuals, members of a team, and part of a broader learning community.

Taking an external look. The external perspective begins on the very first afternoon, with a key stakeholder's view—that of shareholders. The module called "How the Street Analyzes Weyerhaeuser" is aimed at helping participants understand who Weyerhaeuser's shareholders are, how capital markets assess the value of companies, and how "the Street" currently views Weyerhaeuser.

Participants get a chance to interact with another key external stakeholder: customers. Several of Weyerhaeuser's key customers spend an entire day with participants in WLI. Together they learn about, consider, and identify implications of global business forces, trends, and strategy. Weyerhaeuser executives ask their key customers what they believe will be the key distinguishing characteristics of the company that will be the industry leader in three to five years.

The external perspective addresses the role of competitors. Participants work in teams, assuming the role of the top management team of four different competitors. Using their own experience with these competitors, plus a presession reading brief, participants are asked (in their role of acting as their competition's top management team) to develop a winning strategy for the next three to five years.

Following their role-playing work, participants discuss with faculty and each other what these potential competitor strategies and scenarios might mean for Weyerhaeuser. At the end of that day the executives are asked to work in subgroups to identify the most important implications of what they learned in this session, both for Weyerhaeuser and for themselves as leaders. Each team presents their findings to the other teams, with the process resulting in a summary of the best ideas from the full group.

Taking an introspective look. Participants' introspection begins on the very first evening as the faculty begins the process of building the group of participants into a strong learning community. The intent of this module is understanding how we learn and how to avoid typical pitfalls in the learning process.

Participants are led through a process in which they agree on principles for how they want to work and learn together. These are posted in the classroom and in each room where subgroups meet and are referred to throughout the entire program to ensure all are living by those principles.

Participating executives have the opportunity to take an in-depth look at themselves through the use of the Myers-Briggs Type Indicator (MBTI)®. This segment goes beyond just receiving and analyzing one's personal MBTI scores. Participants get to better understand themselves and others, to know why individual differences are important, and to learn how to appreciate and leverage these differences. Particular emphasis is placed on the implications of what they have learned for leadership and teamwork.

Executives also get feedback on the Weyerhaeuser Roadmap Leadership Competencies' 360-degree feedback instrument and process, with these objectives:

- Help individual participants understand their strengths as well as areas of needed improvement
- Create an improvement action plan
- Know how to follow up back on the job to optimize performance
- Set individual and team learning goals for the upcoming simulation

After hearing a faculty presentation on the genesis and purpose of the Weyerhaeuser Roadmap Leadership 360-degree feedback instrument, participants are briefed on how to analyze their feedback report. They can then meet one-on-one with an external feedback specialist for guidance on interpreting their feedback and drafting their action plans for tracking progress after WLI. Participants are briefed on how to follow up back on the job to ensure positive results.

Managing the Roadmap for Success: The Business Simulation. The broad objectives for the part of Week One that includes the custom-designed simulation include the following:

- Developing the leadership capabilities needed to use the Roadmap to grow the business profitably
- Knowing how to generate profits using the Roadmap
- Developing a deep understanding of the Roadmap and being able to create that understanding in others
- Building a strong sense of ownership of the Roadmap

Facilitators conduct the interactive Weyerhaeuser Roadmap business simulation with participants over the course of three days. As shown in Figure 7.2, the simulation helps participants learn experientially how the Roadmap processes impact Weyerhaeuser's key business goals—for example, return on net assets (RONA) greater than 17 percent.

Figure 7.2. Business Simulation Components.

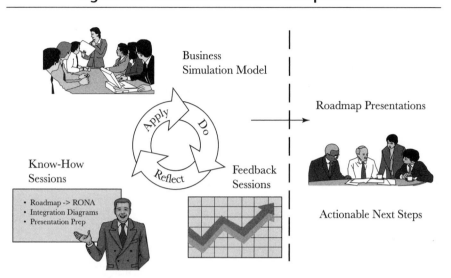

Participants work in five teams. Each team manages a simulated business and competes against the other teams to achieve the highest RONA while utilizing the Roadmap. The simulation encompasses three years of experience. After each simulated year, the facilitators report the results and identify key learning points. Following the simulation, the facilitators lead an application workshop in which participants identify how they will incorporate what they have learned into their everyday jobs to improve business performance.

The rich lessons about the Roadmap learned from the simulation are mined during in-depth debriefings about the experience. These debriefings also provide participants with a better understanding of effective leadership and high-performance teams, as well as how to work more effectively in future team situations. The facilitator links back to the MBTI along with their principles for group learning, getting participants to evaluate their experience working as a team during the simulation—basically, what went well and what could have been done better. Individual participants also identify two or three specific ways in which they can make their next team experiences back home more effective.

Commitment to a Course of Action. It is absolutely critical for continued success and progress after the formal program that participants use a structured follow-through process for transfer of learning and application on the job. We have found over the years that no matter how well designed, well delivered, and successful an executive development experience may be, without significant support and structure for the transfer and application of learning, the best intentions often go awry.

The second-to-last module of Week One of WLI focuses directly on the follow-through process. It gives participants an opportunity to consider what additions or modifications to make to their action plans, focusing on what will lead to leadership growth.

At this time, the facilitator leads a discussion on the importance and power of follow-through. Individuals review the key insights and knowledge gained during Week One, using a WLI learning journal in which they have been making daily entries. They identify the two key goals or action plans for which they are going to hold themselves accountable. They work in groups of three to share their goals and action plans and give each other ideas for improving them.

Each class appoints a leader who will have responsibility for reporting progress on action plans to the WLI manager. All participants are expected to review their action plans with their managers upon returning to work. Simulation teams are responsible for managing their progress, coaching each other, and providing progress updates to their class leader.

WLI Week Two: Inspired Leaders Inspiring Others. The objectives for Week Two, which takes place three months after the end of Week One, are

- Learning how to sponsor innovation that is focused on key targets
- Discussing how to achieve both one company (acting as a single company instead of as independent business units) and innovation
- Improving leadership effectiveness by learning and experiencing the four critical demands of leadership:
  - Setting and communicating direction
  - Creating alignment
  - Setting and living values
  - Growing and developing self and others
- Creating specific plans for building the Weyerhaeuser leadership of the future

Week Two launches with an opportunity for participants to work in the same groups created at the end of Week One. These groups review progress on their action plans, discussing what worked and what didn't as well as providing advice to each other.

The Leader's Role in Sponsoring Focused Innovation. In the first full day of Week Two participants tackle the topic of "The Leader's Role in Sponsoring Focused Innovation." The intent of this segment is to help participants better understand how innovation really happens in organizations, and to know the key roles people play in the innovation process. Participants also learn how to sponsor innovation and *intrapreneurs*—a term coined by Gifford Pinchot in his book *Intrapreneuring,* in which he defined intrapreneurs as "dreamers who do"—those individuals who take hands-on responsibility for creating innovation of any kind within an organization. The intrapreneur may be the creator or inventor, but is always the "dreamer who figures out how to turn an idea into a profitable reality."

Participants are instructed how to keep innovation efforts focused and grounded in key strategic priorities and targets. They are also assisted in understanding and improving the climate for innovation that currently exists in their area of Weyerhaeuser. Part of this entails wrestling with the sometimes conflicting concepts of one company versus the appropriate business unit independence that may be required to be innovative.

The faculty presentation that takes place during the session debunks current myths about the innovation process. Faculty members delineate the realities of how innovation occurs, explaining the five stages of innovation:

- Call to adventure
- Finding your path
- Walking the road between trials and revelations
- Breakthrough (receiving the boon)
- Offering your gift to the world

The Four Demands of Leadership. Just as the simulation was the center of Week One, the Four Demands of Leadership session serves as the centerpiece for Week Two.

The Four Demands of Leadership session begins with a brief history of the study of leadership and the origins of the four demands (introduced in the Chapter Six case study of First Bank of Sweden). Research and writing on leadership points to four common things that all corporate leaders have to do well:

- Set and communicate direction
- Create alignment among key constituencies
- Set and live values
- Grow and develop self and others

For each of these four demands, participants are presented with an interactive case that illustrates that demand (an article, video, case study, or the like). Then, working in small groups, participants identify and share their best practices for each demand. The full group then identifies the "best of the best" practices.

Participants engage in a learning lab—an experiential exercise in which they have a chance to practice the demand. They then have a debriefing based on how their lab experience compared with what was learned in the "case" and their discussion of best practices. Participants are then able to individually modify their goals and action plans based on what they learned.

During one evening participants engage in a process called *personal leadership stories.* The objective is for participants to reflect back on and identify the events and people that shaped their beliefs and values and that had an impact on the kind of person and leader that they have become. They have the opportunity to craft personal stories, each story expressing the participant's innermost beliefs about his or her identity as a leader. Participants share their stories with a small peer group and then identify collective themes revealed by them. This exercise allows participants to learn more about themselves and each other.

The Four Demands of Leadership segment takes place over the course of two days in the middle of Week Two. The objective is to enhance the leadership effectiveness of participants by helping them understand what the four demands are, experiencing each demand, sharing best practices, and improving their leadership effectiveness.

Building Tomorrow's Team. The participant-led Building Tomorrow's Team session engages individuals and teams in developing perspectives on the challenges, skills, and talent attraction and retention strategies needed for the future success of Weyerhaeuser. Participants are asked to develop individually, and then as small teams, their thoughts on the following:

- Key challenges to building tomorrow's team
- Identifying future skills, talents, and demographics
- Retaining critical talent

Beginning with background information about the state of the company's workforce, teams are asked to prepare a presentation to answer one of these questions:

- What is expected of Weyerhaeuser leaders when we say, "Leaders have the responsibility to build tomorrow's team"?
- What are the critical tools, skills, and resources at our disposal that we should use to select and retain critical talent?
- What do we, as leaders, need to do regarding diversity in the next three to seven years, and why?
- What are the things a person really needs to do to get ahead as a leader in the company, and what responsibility do we have to develop our people into leaders?
- What are the critical challenges facing us in attracting the kind of talent and skills we will need in the next three to five years and beyond, and what are the most important steps that company leaders at all levels can take to meet these challenges?

Following the Building Tomorrow's Team segment, there is a major shifting of gears as the broader theme of inspired leaders inspiring others is brought to the fore. This is when the Performance Edge module is experienced. Participants learn to better understand the role of trust, courage, and the notion of stretch goals in effective leadership, with the object of improving their own skills in these arenas. This leadership lab allows participants to experience viscerally the effect of trust, courage, and stretch goals in an outdoor high-ropes challenge course.

Afterward, the faculty leads participants in a debriefing on their overall experience to ensure the transfer of what they learned to the improvement of their leadership skills back home.

Consistent with the week's theme of inspired leaders inspiring others, the morning of the last day of Week Two focuses on peer feedback. This segment seeks to give participants some practice giving and receiving feedback and to help them understand their strengths and how to leverage them.

This involves real-time feedback between peers. During the week, each participant closely observes one of his or her peers in preparation for leading the group's observations about that person during the feedback module. In small groups, in "fishbowl" style, each participant receives feedback on his or her strengths. Participants also plan how they will more effectively leverage their strengths back on the job.

Following their peer feedback session, participants have the opportunity to shift their perspective from real-time, specific personal behaviors into the future. The Creating Our Future module helps participants formulate a clear vision of what kind of company they want to create, and to generate ideas about what it will take to achieve that vision.

The participants take time to update their goals and action plans with what they've learned. The program concludes with a rousing closing ceremony that celebrates the new Weyerhaeuser that will result from application of what they've learned.

Afterthoughts

It should be noted that over time WLI has evolved—faculty have changed, modules have been modified or dropped, hot-button issues morphed—and like any living organism the program is kept alive through this dynamic process of change.

One of the changes took place when Parker retired and John Garrison became the new director of strategic education. One of John's early observations regarding WLI was this:

"It's been said 'the ability to learn faster than our competitors may be the only sustainable competitive advantage in the 21st century.' [Arie DeGeus] The Weyerhaeuser Leadership Institute plays an important part in energizing us to become a learning organization.

"WLI is a forum for bringing the best of our varied cultures together to build the Weyerhaeuser for tomorrow. The relationships that are built here will serve to help us all think beyond our individual businesses to truly become one company."

Results

John's manager, Ed Rogel, executive vice president of human resources, attended WLI personally. In the WLI newsletter he reminisced about WLI in general and his personal experience:

Developing leaders is one of the highest priorities for our company—not only in the next few years because of impending retirements, but continuously. A company that grows its leaders will be competitive in this changing global marketplace. WLI is our major thrust for developing our top 500 leaders. From WLI Class Two I remember the shared challenges and learnings and the huge benefit from blending people across all geographies, businesses and functions and, yes, several companies—Weyerhaeuser, Willamette, McMillan Bloedel, Trus Joist, Cavenham, Dierks, P&G and more.

One of my favorite parts of WLI is the downstream effect. Think of it: Five hundred leaders, who, through WLI goals, improve things on behalf of their customers . . . or sharing lessons from WLI with our own leadership groups. Right now, Mark Starnes of Recycling [department] is gearing up for a mini-WLI led by his leadership team. Carl Chapman, Alan Sherrington and J. R. Roth recently sponsored a two-day Roadmap simulation adapted for the Atlantic lumber business. Class 8 took on a class project on improving vertical and horizontal integration among businesses.

CEO Steve Rogel's strong sponsorship of the WLI remains evident throughout the various WLI sessions. Senior management team (SMT) members visit each class to share the vision for Weyerhaeuser. SMT members fully participate in WLI as students and as faculty. SMT members act as follow-up sponsors, monitoring participants' progress on their action plans, and holding periodic reviews of results.

Both CEO Rogel and Weyerhaeuser's SMT serve as role models for WLI themes— they strive very hard to practice what WLI preaches. The SMT "owns" and uses WLI to drive the transformation of Weyerhaeuser.

Chick Sandifer, WLI project leader, noted that the internal newsletter was created to share "how far we've journeyed and how far there is to go." In that newsletter Steve Rogel wrote the following:

Weyerhaeuser Leadership Institute has generated exceptionally positive reactions and I am confident that WLI will continue to positively influence our financial performance and competitive position.

When WLI started, my hopes were for a common set of learnings and experiences that would challenge and develop our leadership across the company. Now, a little more than halfway through . . . we have accomplished what we desired through better understanding and actions related to the Roadmap for Success, through better understanding about Wall Street and global business trends, through improved understanding and learning from our leaders from other companies like MB, TJ and Willamette, and, of course, through growth of individual and team leadership skills.

Summary

The Weyerhaeuser Leadership Institute case (see Table 7.1 for the program at a glance) is an excellent example of how executive development can be used both

Table 7.1. Weyerhaeuser Leadership Institute Program at a Glance.

Participants	Top 500 executives
Theme	One Company, with inspiring leaders aligned around the Roadmap
Objectives	• Develop critical leadership capabilities to grow the business safely and profitably • Accelerate the "New Weyerhaeuser" cultural change to speed, simplicity, and decisiveness • Orient new leaders from other cultures (acquired companies) to the company's vision, values, and strategies • Create a cadre of diverse leadership talent that will be a source of competitive advantage • Help leaders capture the true business value of a streamlined one-company approach • Develop the capabilities to provide inspiring leadership to employees and create excitement and positive energy in their organizations about the company's future
Content	• Segment One: Building alignment around Weyerhaeuser's Roadmap • Taking an external look • Segment Two: Inspired Leaders Inspiring Others • "Intrapreneurship" segment • Five Stages of Innovation • The Four Demands of Leadership • Personal leadership stories • Building Tomorrow's Team
Length	Two six-day "weeks" over a three-month period
Frequency	Four or five per year
Class Size and Mix	Groups of 25, mix of many different parts of the Weyerhaeuser business
Faculty	Senior management team, external experts
Location	Vancouver, British Columbia, and San Diego, California

as a catalyst for a major organizational change and to build the new capabilities identified as critical to achieving the transformation.

Next Up:

In Chapter Eight, we discuss Weyerhaeuser in an earlier time period, confronting one of the most critical of all business issues—survival. Suffice it to say, Weyerhaeuser met that challenge with flying colors.

CHAPTER EIGHT

IDENTIFYING AND ADDRESSING CRITICAL BUSINESS CHALLENGES

Every business will face, at some point, a set of important business issues, opportunities, and challenges. Some are external—perhaps focused on the marketplace, such as responding to new customer or regulatory requirements or addressing competitive threats. Others are internal challenges—for example, improving time to market or accelerating new business innovation. Often an issue is mission-critical and pervasive, and therefore needs to be addressed companywide.

Case Study: The Weyerhaeuser Forest Products Company

In Chapter Seven we discussed the Weyerhaeuser Leadership Institute as a case example of how executive development was used to help with a major organizational transformation. In this chapter we again use Weyerhaeuser as a case in point. The story in Chapter Seven dealt with the transformation of the entire company; now we will spin the tale of how one of the three business units in Weyerhaeuser, the Forest Products Company (FPC) (the other business units were the Paper Company and Real Estate), addressed a challenge to its very existence.

About the Company

With the exception of the U.S. federal government, Weyerhaeuser is the largest landowner in North America. Primarily a natural resources company, it has historically been able to harvest trees wherever and whenever it wanted to. The company has been able to sell trees and their byproducts very profitably.

For the better part of the company's first three-quarters of a century, Weyerhaeuser had little significant competition for its core businesses. This situation resulted, as such situations often can, in FPC becoming known as arrogant, overconfident, bloated, bureaucratic, and hard to do business with.

But FPC's success soon drew the eye of competitors, the likes of which Weyerhaeuser had never seen before: nonunion, smaller companies that tended to be much leaner and more nimble than the septuagenarian. These were mostly owner-operated companies with low cost structures that allowed them to be both responsive and quick-moving in the marketplace.

Their size and cost structure made their pricing fiercely competitive—and the profit margins of this new breed of competitor tended to be higher. Unlike larger, more established companies, which simply sold the customer a tree or lumber, these new competitors offered specialized products for particular market niches to meet specific customer needs. Even in an industry with overcapacity, this customer-focused, value-added dimension made the products of the new breed of competitor more marketable as well as more profitable than FPC's.

These owner-operated upstarts also tended to be very hungry and aggressive and highly motivated.

The Challenge

FPC was particularly vulnerable to this new type of competitor. FPC had approximately half of Weyerhaeuser's employees and two-thirds of its revenues, and its only real competitors before the emergence of this new breed were other large companies like itself, such as Georgia-Pacific, Boise Cascade, and Champion International. They tended to compete on price. FPC was still operating primarily with a commodity mind-set.

In addition to the situation of emerging competitors, the forest products industry as a whole was severely impacted by a wrenching recession. Being part of a cyclical industry, FPC was accustomed to the turbulence of the marketplace. But the one-two punch of the recession and this new breed of competitors left FPC reeling and sorely in need of a major organizational rebuilding. Morale was low and turnover, historically low, was on the rise.

At the crisis point, FPC's performance was in the bottom quartile for the industry compared with its competitors in virtually every category, and employee morale was at an all-time low. Weyerhaeuser had tried everything to turn the company around: they had laid off 25 percent of the workforce, frozen hiring, eliminated layers of management, and taken many other drastic measures.

The challenge for FPC was described quite colorfully by its CEO, Charley Bingham, as a "blue funk." Speaking plainly, this is a case example of the most critical business challenge of all—survival.

Thinking strategically, the CEO decided that FPC needed to shift from being a producer of raw materials or commodities to being a marketer of specialized products. He believed the way to do this was to differentiate their products in such a way that the company added an extraordinary value for their customers. He saw the scale of this change as huge and far-reaching.

Over the course of the next few years, the CEO wanted to reverse the existing percentage of sales dollars from 80 percent commodity products and 20 percent differentiated products to 80 percent differentiated products and 20 percent commodity products. At corporate, Weyerhaeuser had initiated a massive reorganization and moved as quickly as it could from a very centralized organization to a very decentralized one. More decision-making was pushed down to the three business units, one of which was FPC.

The restructuring and reorganization were important steps, but FPC's ability to implement its new strategic direction was undercut by the corrosively poor morale and increasing pessimism about the possibility of sustained future success (the "blue funk"). Theoretically FPC was positioned for success with the new structure, consisting of dozens of profit centers, each largely responsible for its own bottom line. The question was whether FPC could actually become more responsive to the marketplace and generate better profit margins from specialties rather than commodities.

The Solution

Bingham and his senior team realized that for FPC to ultimately succeed, a complete rebuilding was required. "We had to change the whole way we thought about the business . . . from being a raw-materials manufacturing organization—which characterized us in all our history—to being primarily a customer- and market-driven organization." The two hundred profit centers that resulted from the reorganization needed leaders capable of running a total business profitably. FPC also needed leaders who could shift their focus externally to the customer and the marketplace—and who understood the complexities of "value" to the customer—what it was, how to create it, and how to use it to gain and maintain a competitive advantage. One thing Bingham knew for sure: he needed a way to revitalize and reenergize the organization!

Although Bingham saw these needs as being critical, he wanted to avoid rushing into a quick fix. His goal was not just to convince the senior team about the strategic change required; rather, he wanted the whole organization to buy into the new strategic direction. With this in mind, he went to his head of human resources, Ed Rogel—whom we met in the last chapter—and to the head of organization/executive development, Horace Parker. Bingham asked them to design a formal leadership development program—a high-quality intervention with which they could address the critical issues facing the organization and revitalize FPC.

These were the goals for the leadership development effort:

- Build the mind-sets and skills needed to lead the company into the future
- Equip leaders with the business acumen needed to run a business unit profitably and, just as important, make them act like owners
- Become much more market- and customer-focused
- Overcome the morale problems (the "blue funk") and build excitement about the future of the company

The CEO formulated three criteria for the effort that soon became known as the Leadership Institute. He told Parker, who was given the assignment of heading up the Institute:

- We need quality
- [We need] something that is innovative in the learning process to "grab" participants' attention—to jolt them out of their familiar ways of thinking about the business
- All the learning has to be applicable and directly transferable to the job

Parker remembers how daunting this task seemed. He recalls going into his office one December afternoon, shortly after getting the call to action, and finding a file full of articles that Rogel had dumped on his desk. Close to the top of the pile was our 1985 *Harvard Business Review* article "Tailor Executive Development to Strategy." After reading it, Parker called us and said that he believed FPC needed to do a lot of what was outlined in the article on strategic use of executive development. Two days later one of us flew out to Seattle to begin working with Parker and Rogel on a concept and proposal for this leadership development intervention.

The FPC Leadership Institute Is Born. Right from the start, we all knew that senior executive support and commitment for the Leadership Institute were critical to its success—and initially, to its survival. A steering committee, consisting mostly of senior line executives representing a broad cross-section of FPC, was formed to guide the overall project. This was early in the research and needs analysis process (see Step One in Chapter Two). After completing interviews with a cross-section of about thirty leaders from all parts of FPC, the steering committee would help analyze and identify capability gaps and development needs among FPC executives.

The steering committee was also responsible for making certain that the program would be tailored to FPC's specific needs and not turn out to be some "ivory tower" exercise. They would serve as watchdogs, monitoring progress and seeing to it that the program stayed on track and was totally relevant.

The results of our needs assessment identified several critical capability needs, including strengthening leadership skills, learning to lead a customer-focused organization, enhancing innovation and creativity, and building the financial skills to run a profitable business. The specific objectives of the Leadership Institute, approved by the steering committee, are listed in Exhibit 8.1.

The Leadership Institute consisted of four weeklong sessions delivered over the course of twelve months. In the four months in between sessions, the participants

Exhibit 8.1. Leadership Institute Objectives.

- Create unity of purpose and commitment to FPC's vision, values, and principles
- Build a market/customer-driven enterprise
- Improve leadership skills and instill a sense of responsibility for leading FPC into the future
- Develop a broad business perspective and ownership attitudes and competencies
- Become more creative and innovative in running the business
- Improve communication, cooperation, and a sense of teamwork across business unit and functional lines

implemented the personal action plans they had created at the end of the session week, aimed at applying what they had learned. They also had assignments to prepare them for the next week, plus they worked in small groups on team projects that required applying what they learned in a form of action learning.

Exhibit 8.2 shows the overall architecture of the Leadership Institute.

Week One: The Leadership Challenge. Week One focused on the critical leadership issues faced by FPC. The objectives of the first week included

- Developing a strong sense of what leadership is and its importance and role in shaping and guiding FPC
- Understanding what is required to improve personal leadership effectiveness and acquiring the knowledge and commitment to do so
- Developing a strong sense of teamwork, unity of purpose, and esprit de corps
- Understanding top management's vision of FPC's future

Exhibit 8.2. Leadership Institute Architecture.

Week 1	The Leadership Challenge
Personal action planning	Assignments and team projects
Week 2	Creating and leading a customer/ market-driven enterprise
Personal action planning	Assignments and team projects
Week 3	Developing our capabilities and creativity
Personal action planning	Assignments and team projects
Week 4	Leading the charge—running a total business
The "beginning"	

This first week's session was intended to jar participants out of their traditional ways of thinking—to get them to see leadership and teamwork in new and different ways. Experiential learning was one method that was used. Participants engaged in intense leadership development experiences, including a unique combination of Socratic dialogue and outdoor leadership challenges. A typical outdoor challenge would require teams to use their leadership and team skills in a task for which they didn't have the technical skills to solve the problem; for example, a simulation of transporting an injured hiker off a mountain peak.

Each outdoor leadership challenge was preceded by brief instruction on a leadership model, which participants immediately applied in the challenging experience, followed by an in-depth debriefing of what had been learned and how it could be applied back on the job.

Referring to great works of literature read by the participants as presession work, the faculty led Socratic discussions on values and their impact on leadership and the participants as individual leaders.

Again, for the purposes of executive development, action learning refers to working in teams on real business problems or opportunities for development purposes. As shown in Exhibit 8.2, immediately after the first week, participants worked on team projects in action learning teams to address critical business issues faced by FPC, applying the leadership lessons they had just learned.

The approximately six participants in each action learning team chose their project based on a significant business problem or opportunity they believed was important and would benefit from the application of the knowledge and skills they had learned during Week One.

Each participant established a personal action development plan containing two or three leadership behaviors the participant wanted to improve during the four months that would pass before Week Two of the Institute was held. There were other assignments participants needed to complete during the interim to prepare for Week Two, such as being sensitive to and aware of their behaviors that either support or undermine the goals and values of a customer- and market-driven organization.

As Exhibit 8.2 shows, executive health and fitness was a theme throughout the entire program. The Institute encouraged participants to set up personal fitness goals to work on throughout the program. Each person had the opportunity in Week One to receive a complete health exam and create a guided fitness plan to follow during the year of the Institute. Every morning included optional fitness classes; although the Institute moved to a different venue for each of the four weeks of the program, the facilities always included a fitness facility and professional trainers. There were also special courses available throughout on such topics as heart disease and nutrition. At the end of the Institute, one participant wrote in his evaluation, "You saved my life."

Week Two: Creating and Leading a Customer- and Market-Driven Enterprise. The guiding theme of Week Two was leading a customer- and market-focused organization. During this second week, executives from FPC worked hand in hand with their peers from major customer organizations to apply concepts, tools, and frameworks to their real-time working relationship.

The customer was central to FPC's new strategic focus—a major change from the company's historic patterns. Customers were an integral part of the program for a full three to four days during Week Two. FPC had CEOs, presidents, and product managers from their top one hundred customers participate side by side with them in the Institute. Each week, four peer-level executives from major customers attended along with the twenty-four or so Weyerhaeuser participants.

With their customers as learning partners, FPC executives focused on

- Becoming customer- and market-driven
- How the industry and marketplace are changing and what should be expected in the future
- Determining what customers want and why
- Forging profitable partnerships with customers by delivering superior value at a profit
- Assessing and improving FPC's corporate culture in relation to becoming a customer- and market-driven enterprise

On a typical day, the morning would include content presented by world-class faculty. In the afternoon, small groups made up of six FPC executives and one customer would apply what they learned to that customer's specific situation. This was a far cry from the more traditional, academic way of learning about becoming customer-focused—say, by studying case studies of Ford Motor Company. This was learning in real time, with live ammunition.

At the end of their sessions with customers, FPC executives forged action plans that would allow them to continue applying what they learned toward the creation of more profitable partnerships with each customer. The goal was to define ways in which the company and its key customers could work together so that they would both be more profitable. A bonus result of this interaction was a powerful bonding experience between the FPC executives and their customers.

Week Three: Developing Our Capabilities and Creativity. There were four major objectives for Week Three:

- Checking and reviewing progress on becoming customer- and market-oriented and determining what more needs to be done
- Understanding how to be personally more creative and how to stimulate creativity on the job
- Understanding the Weyerhaeuser Excellent Executive model, and receiving feedback on personal strengths as well as areas for improvement
- Developing plans for improving personal leadership capability and creativity

Week Three was targeted at developing creativity, innovation, and leadership skills. Participants received feedback from their manager, peers, and those who worked for them (360-degree feedback) on their leadership values and practices. At the end of Week One they had received a draft of the profile of the Weyerhaeuser Excellent Executive—the specific activities and behaviors that the leader would demonstrate if he or she were living the desired values and displaying the expected leadership practices. In Week One they had the opportunity to make recommendations for enhancements to the draft. The draft was then turned into a leadership feedback instrument so that in Week Three participants could receive 360-degree feedback. This customized leadership inventory used by FPC for 360-degree feedback was referred to as the Excellent Executive model—an articulation of the values and leadership practices expected of FPC leaders.

To illustrate, the two major components of FPC's Excellent Executive model are outlined as follows:

Serving the customer. The Excellent Executive

- Knows who his or her customers are
- Is dedicated to meeting the needs of people who use the company's services or products
- Encourages and listens to input from customers
- Acts to solve customers' problems in a timely manner

Building customer importance. The Excellent Executive

- Consistently treats the users of the company's products or services as a top priority
- Clearly communicates the importance of these people
- Demands that customers be spoken of with respect and discourages negative comments about them within the company
- Is more committed to customers' long-term satisfaction than to the company's short-term gain

The Spouse Program. Week Three encouraged creativity and innovation through lectures, discussion, and application exercises.

One of the unique aspects of the institute and a demonstration of creativity and innovation was the spouse program. Parker was the father of this idea. Given the significance of the Leadership Institute and the level of effort and commitment FPC now expected of its executives, Parker thought it was essential to engage the participants' spouses in a meaningful way. Initially, the idea was to have executives joined by their spouses for a day at the Institute. Then Parker got the idea of creating a team made up of participants' spouses and asking *them* to design the spouse component of the program. Parker's wife Kathy was part of the design team that decided that spouses should

- Know more about the company and their spouse's role within it
- Have a program within the Leadership Institute specifically designed for them
- Have a leadership development experience themselves
- Have fun

The resulting program included spouses for the entire five days of Week Three. For half of that time, spouses participated in segments with their partners. The other half consisted of sessions reserved exclusively for spouses. They basically participated in a mini-version of the Institute, including such things as the outdoor team-building experience and the business simulation. There was also a special event to recognize the contribution of spouses to the success of the program.

Over the life span of the Leadership Institute, the CEO of Weyerhaeuser received over two hundred letters from spouses saying, among many other things, that they now had a much better and deeper understanding of the company and its goals and what was expected of their spouses and why.

Week Four: Leading the Charge—Running a Total Business. Everything was brought together in the Institute's final week—leadership skills, customer focus, and innovation. This part of the program served as a sort of final exam for FPC executives. They now had to take everything they'd learned and apply it to running a total business.

The metaphorical bow that tied it all together was a course in financial management from an entrepreneurial perspective—how to run a profit-loss center and make money. The objectives for Week Four were to send executives on their way with

- Skill and confidence to run their part of the business as if it were their own (that is, as if it were owner-operated and utterly entrepreneurial)
- Understanding about how to run a total business—not just one component of a larger company—profitably
- A strong sense of teamwork in confronting their challenges and opportunities
- Assimilation and application of lessons learned from the Leadership Institute to optimize commitment, confidence, and inspiration

After acquiring the financial essentials for operating a total business profitably, participants engaged in a competitive business simulation that pulled together all the elements of Week Four. This computer simulation was filled with financial variables the FPC executives needed to understand and master. The experience of running the business as the top management team for several years of operation was condensed into two days. The software for this simulation included all the opportunities and constraints existing in the real forest products industry as teams competed for customers and profits. To "win," teams had to successfully apply all the key lessons from the four weeks of the leadership institute.

As their final experience together, participants were asked to write and deliver a speech. The scenario called for them to prepare to give the commencement address at the Harvard Business School, the Institut Européen d'Administration des Affaires (INSEAD), or their favorite business school three years from the last day of the program. The subject for the address was to be "How the Weyerhaeuser Forest Products Company Became Such an Incredible Success." Executives were also to speak about their role in making it happen.

Individual executives first worked by themselves on the task, then shared their speeches in four small teams. The teams, in turn, collaborated on a skit that compiled the best ideas from all the individual speeches. Seeing all of the skits gave participants the chance to compare visions of what the future might look like for FPC, what it would take to get there, and what their contribution could be in the long term.

The exercise also provided the executives with an opportunity to envision what success might look and feel like later, when they'd been able to apply what they learned at the Institute. The skits gave top management and the executives themselves an exciting, visceral vision of FPC's future.

Results

The participants in the first Institute were the CEO and his top team of twenty executives. The CEO was the primary champion for the Institute. His attendance at each and every Week One sent a powerful signal to the top management of FPC and to the whole organization about the importance of the Institute and of leadership development as well.

Initially, there was a great deal of resistance to the Institute. Executives argued that it would demand too much of their time. Taking four weeks away from their time at work when things were as dire as they were made no sense at all to many of the executives who were slated to be involved. The cost to design and deliver the Institute seemed to be a staggering sum.

The CEO "provided critical air cover," as Horace Parker described it, during the early months of the Institute. Parker was convinced that once the quality of the Institute became clear and some early successful results were realized, the resistance would melt away.

He was right. Shortly after the Institute got up and running, and the projects launched as a consequence of the Institute began to bear fruit, massive resistance turned into enthusiastic demand for the program. What was initially to be for only the top 200 executives ultimately saw 1,500 total participants.

Exhibit 8.3 identifies some of the outcomes attributed to the FPC Leadership Institute. Horace Parker identified an additional successful outcome: "We showed Weyerhaeuser that we could successfully use executive development to drive business improvement and results!"

Given the intended outcomes of the Leadership Institute, the results listed in Exhibit 8.3 are more than gratifying in and of themselves. But they don't tell the whole story of the Institute's success. When asked about their view of their own

Exhibit 8.3. WLI Results.

- Dramatic increase in teamwork/collaboration
- 250 projects = resulting in more than $50 million in improvements
- Competitive performance from third to first quartile
- 23% increase in customer revenues
- Rated first in customer satisfaction among competitors

personal gains resulting from their participation in the Institute, FPC executives most frequently identified

- Stronger leadership skills
- An increase in teamwork and group participation
- Improved working relationships with subordinates, including better communication, particularly in giving and receiving feedback
- Skills in coaching, providing autonomy and giving positive reinforcement
- Focus on customer service, satisfaction and relations

Summary

In total, we believe the FPC Leadership Institute serves as an excellent example of how executive development can be used to both identify and address critical business challenges facing a major corporation in complex times. Table 8.1 shows the program at a glance.

Next Up:

An issue that perplexes many people is whether or not the impact of executive development can be measured. In Chapter One we noted that many companies say they will need to but also say they are not good at it. Chapter Nine presents evidence that we can—with descriptions of ten approaches and the results realized.

Table 8.1. Weyerhaeuser Forest Products Company Program at a Glance.

Participants	Initially the top 200 executives, then top 1,500
Themes	• The Leadership Challenge • Creating and leading a customer- and market-driven enterprise • Developing our capabilities and creativity • Leading the charge—running a total business
Objectives	• Create unity of purpose and commitment to FPC's vision, values, and principles • Build a customer- and market-driven enterprise • Improve leadership skills and instill a sense of responsibility for leading FPC into the future • Develop a broad business perspective and ownership attitudes and competencies • Become more creative and innovative in running the business • Improve communication, cooperation, and a sense of teamwork across unit lines
Content	(See Themes)
Length	Four weeklong sessions over a twelve-month period
Frequency	Eight to ten sessions started each year
Class Size and Mix	Twenty-five, included segment for spouses
Faculty	CEO, leading university faculty, and consultants, included customers with feedback
Location	Off-site (three different locations)

CHAPTER NINE

THE BUSINESS IMPACT OF CORPORATE EXECUTIVE DEVELOPMENT

Some believe that you can tie executive development to results, some think it's impossible, and some see no point in trying to do so. The good news is that you *can* measure the results of executive development if you want to. In this chapter we will show how various companies have created ways to measure the impact of executive development on both individual and business performance. But let's look at a more basic question first.

Does Development Really Matter?

In our experience, almost all companies espouse the value of executive and leadership development, and more and more are embracing it as central to achieving their strategic objectives. And yet many are still just paying lip service to its value; they remain unconvinced that executive development is critical to their business in any real way.

The resistance we've encountered usually takes the form of one of several arguments:

Leadership development is not fundamental to the bottom line. The economy is doing pretty well. Keeping people employed may become a challenge, but leadership development is not essential.

Leaders are born, not made. Leadership cannot be taught; what *can* be taught are management skills—quantitative and analytical, technical and functional proficiency.

This is the "cream rises to the top" school of thought—but as our friend Morgan McCall from USC is quick to point out, as the cream rises, so does a lot of other garbage.

Leadership development isn't beneficial in the long term. It's nice to do, but not necessary to do—not essential to company strategy.

We agree that corporations need to produce a measurable impact on individual and business performance. But we also believe that leadership development is crucial to the bottom line. In fact, the very factors that have forced businesses to a back-to-basics approach have made executive development more important than ever before. Consider the following:

* *Globalization.* U.S companies no longer unequivocally dominate, as globalization raises the level of worldwide competition, increasing the competition for talent.
* *Diminishing competitive advantages.* Traditional sources of competitive advantage have fallen away. For example, technological innovation is no longer an indicator of supremacy. Government deregulation has made technology less proprietary—it's all too easy to buy technology, making it simpler for more companies to compete in the same markets.
* *Corporate scandals and corruption.* For too many senior executives, leadership is tantamount to abuse of power. Stories of imploding companies filing for bankruptcy or shutting their doors, pictures of corporate officers being led away in handcuffs—these have become all too common.
* *The new war for talent.* We are on the verge of a massive potential movement of employees to new, better jobs. Perhaps companies have been able to get away with not challenging or rewarding their people. Now that the economy is stronger, there are—and will be—more and better job opportunities.

Talent as a Competitive Advantage

All of these factors beg the question, "How can companies stay competitive in this environment?" Talent development may be one of the few remaining areas in which companies can still create a competitive advantage.

"The most important investments we make to keep us ahead in an intensely competitive industry are in the training and education of our people," says Lord Colin Marshall, chairman of British Airways.

Honeywell International Chairman Larry Bossidy says, "I am convinced that nothing we do is more important than hiring and developing people. At the end of the day you bet on people, not on strategies."

Yet there is a palpable sense from progressive CEOs that they don't have the quantity or quality of leaders they need to achieve their growth strategy and take their companies into the next generation of business challenges. And our survey findings, highlighted in Chapter One, clearly indicate that a lack of benchstrength is the number one challenge facing companies today.

"The thing that wakes me up in the middle of the night is not what might happen to the economy or what our competitors might do next," says David Whitman, chairman, president, and CEO of Whirlpool Corporation. "It's worrying about whether we have the leadership talent to implement our new and more complex global strategies."

According to the Center for Creative Leadership, 60 percent of companies agree that leadership development is one of the five factors most critical to their company's success. IBM's Sam Palmisano says this about his company's line of attack: "We don't separate out strategy from leadership." For these leaders and for Palmisano, executive development is not off strategy; it *is* strategy.

This attitude is essential to getting the most out of executive development—and for those companies who wholeheartedly adopt executive development processes, the outcomes have been dramatic. In 1999, Andersen Consulting conducted a study that analyzed business results. Companies with formal leadership development processes in place experienced growth like the following:

- Revenues grew 682 percent compared with 166 percent for companies with little formal leadership development.
- Stock prices grew 901 percent, compared with 74 percent for the other companies.
- Net income growth was 756 percent, compared with a meager 1 percent for companies without formal leadership development.

Chief Executive magazine published a 2003 analysis of the twenty best companies for developing leaders. All put significant resources into their development programs (in the case of IBM, to the tune of $1.1 billion per year), and all these programs had the support of the company's top brass, given more than mere lip service. IBM's Palmisano estimates that he spends 30 percent of his time on development.

Does development matter? What do you think?

Should We Measure the Impact of Executive Development?

So if we've established that executive development does matter, the next question is, should we measure its impact? Interestingly enough, there are arguments both for and against. Jack Welch, the legendary former CEO of General Electric, has been known for championing executive development while arguing against measuring the outcomes. Yet of all the CEOs for whom we have worked in the course of twenty-one years of consulting, not one has asked us to measure the impact of their executive development efforts.

When we raised the issue of measuring the impact of Weyerhaeuser's Leadership Institute under Charlie Bingham, then CEO of the Forest Products Company, Bingham insisted that we not do so. His argument was that if we did an excellent job of identifying their executive development needs and tied them to their marketplace challenges, vision, strategy, and desired transformation, and if we designed a high-quality program and got great faculty to teach it, he was confident that the Institute would meet its objectives. No other measurement of success, Bingham assured us, would be necessary. In other words, he trusted the process.

Bingham's other concern was that if we tried to measure the results, people might become obsessed with the numbers and lose sight of the Institute's real value vis-à-vis its goals.

From a purely theoretical standpoint, we would agree with Bingham; we fully trust in the benefits of executive development and the process, and we don't need to see metrics to be convinced of its value.

However, over the past few years we have changed our view on the question of metrics. We feel strongly that we can and should measure the impact of executive development on both individual and business performance. We have an obligation to do so. Metrics raise the value and importance of our work and the stature of our function. There is no excuse for us to be exempt from the same scrutiny that other strategic investments are under; if we truly believe that we add value, then we shouldn't be afraid of subjecting our efforts to measurement.

From the perspective of anyone campaigning for investing in executive development, or justifying current expenditures, metrics are essential to helping make their case. Not all organizations are spearheaded by visionaries who appreciate the benefits of development. There are those leaders who have to be convinced by a compelling story, one that points directly to the achievement of corporate goals. Metrics also help tell the story to executives, who may or may not be convinced that hours of their personal time can be profitably given over to development.

And for organizations that are experimenting with a mix of development programs—for example, internal and external, classroom, online and coaching—metrics may help them compare the impact of some programs with others.

The following case studies illustrate how some companies measured the results of their development programs. No two sets of metrics are alike; some are very specific and focus on such benchmarks as profits and productivity, while others measure less tangible outcomes. All of them are valuable. (For additional information on measurement methods, see Appendix J, The Different Ways of Measuring Executive Development.)

The Impact of Executive Development—Case Studies

Our experience working with CEOs of major corporations around the world is that most care much less about sophisticated measurements than they do about anecdotal evidence. They know by what they see, hear, and feel whether their executive development efforts are making a difference.

Nevertheless, we have selected a wide variety of cases to illustrate everything from anecdotal evidence to more rigorous metrics. As you'll see in the descriptions that follow, the companies in these case studies all had unique definitions of the outcomes they desired, as well as different agreed-upon criteria for measuring the impact of their programs and processes. These cases are meant to show a wide variety of interesting methods that companies have used to measure impact on leadership effectiveness and business impact, rather than to provide a tutorial on how to conduct measurement.

Ameritech's Network Leadership Development Program (NLDP)

Measuring leadership acumen is hardly an exact science. Still, program administrators for Ameritech's Network Leadership Development Program (NLDP) developed an evaluation strategy for 1,400 managers that would easily tie development to measurable outcomes.[1]

To begin, they determined goals for their one-week program: to improve participants' leadership skills, their productivity and quality, and their ability to manage in a changing and competitive environment.

Next, the team broke down their evaluation strategy into five components: reaction, learning, transfer, results, and return on investment. Each component was matched with one of these indicators of improvement:

Reaction. Participant reaction was measured with evaluation forms given before and after the course. Results here were quite positive: 97 percent of participants agreed with positive statements about the NLDP program.

Learning. Learning was assessed by comparing pre- and post-intervention performance on a work simulation exercise. The results: by the end of the week, 87 percent showed an average 16 percent improvement in the exercise.

1. Dina M. Pasalis, *Human Resource Planning*, "Leading Strategic Change: Tools and Techniques," 1998.

Transfer. Transfer, or the application of concepts to the work environment, was determined by a 360-degree feedback survey performed for each participant. Eighty percent of participants were judged to have improved in the areas of productivity and quality of work.

Results. These were defined as direct effects on the company's bottom line. In this case, the program was responsible for a 17 percent increase in productivity and quality and a reduction in operating costs.

Return on investment. This was determined by comparing the amount of money spent with the amount saved by implementing the post-program changes. All told, Ameritech saved roughly $1.79 for every $1 spent.

BellSouth's Work of Leadership Program

The overall goal of BellSouth's Work of Leadership program was for participants (the top fifty officers at Bell South) to better understand and practice the work of the new BellSouth Leader, a standard that had recently been defined.

The workshop developed by the BellSouth Leadership Institute included two two-day sessions scheduled ten weeks apart. BellSouth wanted their officers to

- Better understand how to integrate services, offerings, and projects across internal boundaries
- Decide upon and implement those actions that most added value to and supported BellSouth's business strategy
- Understand their role as leaders in achieving world-class financial performance

Success was measured by the degree to which the officers could implement a new project that underlined their new emphasis on growing revenues and cutting costs. An action learning exercise—an application that required diverse teams to focus on real business problems or opportunities—was implemented after the first workshop session. Within the ten-week period between sessions, several projects were developed that paid significant, measurable dividends: a new line of business was created, estimated as having a $500 million potential, and one project resulted in $28 million in incremental revenues—far more than offsetting the total cost of the workshop.

In addition to this hard evidence, Melanie Cadenhead, BellSouth's director of executive education, said that the workshop evaluations provided valuable anecdotal evidence of the program's impact:

- "Sessions and projects have highlighted and stimulated cross-entity cooperation."
- "My work with other affiliates has been more open and easier as a result of working together on our project."
- "[The program] created a stronger working relationship with officers."

Even though these outcomes were impossible to quantify, they provided proof enough to BellSouth that these changes would significantly affect the company's future performance. These comments also indicate that BellSouth was addressing a common problem in companies—misalignment among departments—by increasing cross-organization collaboration.

The CalPERS Leadership Challenge

The California Public Employees Retirement System (CalPERS) felt that development was necessary across all levels of its organization. In fact, one of its top five strategic initiatives was called All Staff Training and included everyone from senior executives to unionized staff.

The stated objective of the CalPERS Leadership Challenge was no less daunting a task than to "produce positive, measurable change in leadership behavior." This created a challenge for the CalPERS development team, charged with determining the measurement criteria.

They did this by developing three-day workshops designed to impact all leaders and to be conducted from the top down throughout the organization. The first workshop participants included the CalPERS CEO and his top eleven executives; subsequent workshops were likewise organized by corporate level and calibrated to accommodate their experience level.

A custom-designed 360-degree leadership feedback instrument was created and completed by each participant, their immediate manager, their peers, and the people who reported to them. During the program, participants received confidential feedback on their survey results and one-on-one private coaching. Each participant also created an action plan to both leverage strengths and address areas where they could improve their leadership effectiveness.

To measure the longer-term effectiveness of the program, Keilty, Goldsmith, and Company (now A4SL Coaching) were hired to conduct two progress assessments. These consisted of mini-surveys—the first conducted four months after the workshops, the second four months after that. The surveys went to participants' managers, direct reports, and peers. The most important question on the survey was, "Do you feel this person has become more or less effective as a leader in the past four months?"

Approximately 90 percent of respondents indicated improvement in leadership effectiveness over the first four-month period; 87 percent indicated improvement in the second four-month period.

The use of 360-degree feedback is one of the few ways we have to measure leadership behavior change. A4SL has conducted several extensive before-and-after studies using the clients' full 360-degree feedback instrument to determine perceived change in leadership effectiveness over time (twelve to eighteen months after the initial administration and training). In one study including over eight thousand people in one hundred of the largest companies in the United States, 95 percent of respondents indicated that leadership effectiveness had improved as a result of their executive development experience.

Eastman Kodak's Professional Division, Business Advantage Program

Tying in its leadership development initiative with bottom-line results, Kodak Professional (a division of Eastman Kodak) used a combination of data and anecdotal evidence to determine the success of its Business Advantage Program. The objectives of the program included increasing profitability, improving participants' understanding of the total business and the financial interrelationships of the business, and improving financial performance.

BTS created a customized business simulation and used several levels of evaluation, including participant reaction, learning transfer, results, and return on investment. Responses trended positively: 98 percent of participants rated the program as either very good or excellent; 64 percent reported that their understanding and awareness of the influences that impact profitability was increased by a "great extent."

As for bottom-line impact, the results were solid. Among the remarkable outcomes:

- Product line managers who completed the program reduced inventory on total delivered costs by $30 million
- Participants "found opportunities to reduce assets by up to $500,000"
- One participant "found ways to grow the top line of the business by up to $375,000"
- Participants proved a better understanding of cost of goods sold (COGS) by eliminating costly steps and reducing inventory, saving $3 million
- With four hundred leaders and executives participating in the program at a cost of $1.44 million (including lost productivity, tuition, and travel), and with an estimated $23.4 million return, Kodak Professional estimates return on investment as roughly sixteen to one

GM Links Better Leaders to Better Business

In a 1998 article in *Workforce* magazine,[2] General Motors ranked tenth out of ten in a warehouse/parts suppliers survey.[3] General Motors' Service Parts Organization (SPO) was clearly not meeting its customers' needs. SPO Director Ron Driggert's objective was to improve SPO's culture and business performance.

To determine the rate of success in meeting this objective, a leadership program consisting of a two-day leadership assessment of the senior faculty was implemented as a pilot at one plant only. Each participant in the pilot received individual assessments and a customized leadership development program. Four similar facilities were used as control groups.

The results proved that leadership development was responsible for improvement in both culture and business performance. Productivity improved 21 percent for the pilot group, translating into a $4.4 million savings to operating budget. Comparing

2. "GM Links Better Leaders to Better Business."
3. Steven R. Davis, Jay H. Lucas, and Donald R. Marcotte, 1998.

these savings to the cost of the program—approximately $300,000—the return on investment was fifteen to one.

Other findings that were reported, but not measured, further strengthened the evidence in favor of executive development, including increased health and safety, lower absenteeism, and improved time management.

IBM's Accelerating Change Together (ACT) Initiative

IBM's overall objective was achieving excellence through measurable results, sustainable change, and strong leadership capability. IBM's Accelerating Change Together (ACT) initiative broke down these broad goals into critical business issues that were approached by teams of executives. Within these teams, goals were made more specific, and success became quantifiable.

Pilot Consulting Corporation, which developed ACT for IBM, designed the methodology to attack any business issue. The business impact of using ACT to improve workplace learning and develop leaders has been considerable. In more than four hundred ACT sessions conducted by three hundred internal consultants, the following results have been reported:

- Increased revenue growth of $3.25 billion
- Productivity and overall client savings of $1.2 billion
- Inventory reduction of $565 million
- Market share growth of $3.75 billion

    Anecdotal evidence includes

- Strengthened leadership: making public decisions and using ACT tools to sustain change
- Faster and more disciplined implementation: visible ownership, commitment, monitoring actions
- Enhanced cross-business literacy: strategic alignment, with one voice to the customer
- Improved knowledge management: applying learning cross-functionally

Siemens Nixdorf Information Systems (SNIS) AG Trains Unit Managers to Be Entrepreneurs

Germany's Siemens Nixdorf wanted to develop a new kind of leader, one who could not only sustain business but also grow it.

Professor Neal Thornberry of Babson College, a school best known for its exceptional Center for Entrepreneurship, led the effort to create a customized program for three hundred unit managers. The result was the Entrepreneurial Development Program (EDP), a five-week program conducted in two two-week segments with six to eight weeks allotted in between for application work. The EDP objectives included

- Identification, development, and capture of new business opportunities
- Development of unit managers as corporate entrepreneurs
- Development of general management skills, including finance, marketing, teamwork, and leadership, to help unit managers in implementing new business ventures

During the Entrepreneurial Development Program, unit managers were asked to develop business plans, which they would use to ask the SNIS board for resources.

Assessment of the program's success was mostly anecdotal. A project director of Innovation Initiatives at SNIS reported that in addition to having developed the business plan for Siemens International Venture Capital Program, "The program really helped me understand how venture capital works and how to determine funding and financial returns. It also made me aware of entrepreneurial thinking and how it fits into our environment."

There is one example of a strong financial outcome. Another unit manager used the program concepts to create a unique value proposition for customers; they developed a new client and increased SNIS's revenues by $250 million.

Hewlett-Packard: Dynamic Leadership

When Carly Fiorina took over the helm of HP in 1999, she launched an initiative aimed at reinventing the tech company, whose growth was encumbered by a lack of both alignment and shared purpose.[4]

HP's Workforce Development and Organization Effectiveness Group (WD&OE) designed Dynamic Leadership, the development program meant to integrate the company's reinvention initiative and to achieve the following goals:

- Alignment of Compaq and HP
- Improved collaboration across business units and functional boundaries
- Accelerated raising and resolution of issues
- Improved decision-making

The two-day program included instruction and group exercises and was followed by nine weeks of on-the-job application. Anecdotal evidence and hard data were collected to evaluate the program, including end-of-program evaluations and a three-month post-program financial impact analysis.

More than eight thousand managers have completed Dynamic Leadership, with outstanding results:

- Ninety-four percent of participants reported that they used the program tools to their advantage in the first three months after training, on average 9.5 times

4. Marshall Goldsmith, Dave Ulrich, and Louis Carter, *Best Practice Champions*, "Dynamic Leadership and the Reinvention of HP," Fort Hill Company, 2004.

- Median value per reported application was $3,800—50 percent more than the cost of the program (on an annual basis, that translates to a return on investment ratio of fifteen to one)
- Among the most immediate benefits were reduced decision-making time and realignment with corporate goals
- Among other reported benefits were improved customer service, higher quality, and better morale

Capital One's Coaching Initiative

Capital One wanted to capture the full impact of a burgeoning method of development: executive coaching. Another objective was to determine the value of coaching from within—making managers more responsible for the development of their peers and direct reports.[5]

Data captured from Capital One's study of performance reviews—including coaches, their peers, and their direct reports—made a strong case for the impact of coaching. Those managers who were coached tended to outperform their noncoached peers based on performance appraisal results and promotion rates—and the direct reports of coaches also received more favorable performance reviews and accelerated promotions (this was the big surprise finding!).

According the Stan Horner, head of executive development at the time, the Capital One study provided evidence that coaching resulted in performance improvements not only for the managers coached but also for the people who work for them.

IBM's Basic Blue and The Role of the Manager@IBM

IBM CEO Sam Palmisano wanted a system for helping new managers move into more complex roles. Instead of developing a traditional training program, IBM opted for an ongoing leadership development *process* that equipped its managers to achieve IBM's business strategy.

"We wanted to use [leadership development] to align the organization around the business environment," says Nancy Lewis, vice president, On-Demand Learning for IBM.

The solution was a yearlong, blended-learning program called Basic Blue, in which more than five thousand new managers have participated. A multitiered, highly customized approach is used for managers to track and develop their evolving skills. Instruction includes a weeklong classroom learning lab and three technology-delivered programs. Participants join with their supervisors in guided interactions around real business challenges, in business simulations and individual exercises.

5. Corporate Executive Board, "Capital One: Learning and Development Roundtable Research," 2002.

"The managers become immersed in an orchestrated medley of e-learning, on-the-job, and off-site development. They can engage in learning as it's convenient for them," Lewis says.

A Web-enabled Learning Management System culls 360-degree feedback, supervisor input, and participants' progress in on-line courses to create a customized learning path. One of the elements is Quick Views—best-practice templates for a number of manager functions, such as conducting meetings and providing performance feedback.

IBM estimates the return on investment of Basic Blue to be $450,000 per participant, based on self-reports, 360-degree assessments, and other, less measurable but equally relevant feedback.

"How we [report] goes beyond the generic way of doing the post-survey," says Lewis. "IBM has a different perspective; measurement is not a separate thing . . . [We ask] 'What are your business goals? What leadership skills are needed to get there?' You are on executive score cards, and the [learning] initiative is built from their core measurements."

Although Basic Blue is not an executive-level program, it is highly Web-enabled and we expect future executive programs to move in this direction. We feel this warrants our describing how IBM measures its impact.

Another key IBM initiative, The Role of the Manager@IBM, is clear evidence of the IBM philosophy of "learning as an investment" and, according to Lewis, is measured in the same business context as any other IBM investment. Also sponsored by CEO Sam Palmisano, this program is a huge transformational management development program engaging more than thirty thousand executives and managers. Given the expected cost of $85 million for development and implementation, Lewis felt it was important to hire an outside firm to do an objective evaluation of the effectiveness and business impact. The firm conducted 174 interviews and studied dozens of business cases of how action plans developed in the program had directly impacted business results. They discovered millions of dollars of cost savings, increased revenues, and cost avoidance. In just twelve specific action plans analyzed, $284 million in revenue was achieved.

Table 9.1 presents the essentials of all the executive development programs and results metrics described here.

Summary

It isn't the purpose of this chapter to identify all the possible ways to measure the impact of executive development (see Appendix J for a list of methods used in these cases) or to provide a tutorial on metrics, but rather to make the case that we can and should measure the impact on both individual and business performance. Because when we do, the results can be mighty persuasive!

Table 9.1. The Business Impact of Corporate Executive Development.

Company	Target Training Group	Program Format	Program Objectives	Evaluation Criteria	Program Results
Ameritech Network Leadership Development Program (NLDP)	1400+ managers	1-week course	• Improving leadership skills • Improving ability to manage in a changing and competitive environment • Improving productivity and quality	• Pre- vs. post-intervention performance on work simulation exercise • Participant feedback • 360-degree feedback survey	• 87% showed 16% average improvement on simulation exercise • 97% made positive statements about the program • 17% increase in quality and productivity, reduced operation costs • ROI: $1.79 saved for every $1 spent
BellSouth Work of Leadership Program	Top 50 officers	• Workshop; 2 sessions, 2 days each, 10 weeks in between; 25 officers per session • Action learning involving team projects	To better understand and practice the approach of the new BellSouth leader, by demonstrating the following: • Better understanding of service integration, offerings, and projects across internal boundaries • Implementation of actions that best support BellSouth's business strategy and add the most value • Understanding of role as leaders in achieving world-class financial performance	Extent to which business projects grew revenues and cut costs	• New line of business estimated to earn $500 million • Implementation of project resulting in $28 million incremental revenues Anecdotal evidence: • Stimulated cross-entity cooperation • Work with affiliates more open and easier • Created stronger working relationship with officers

(Continued)

Table 9.1. Continued.

Company	Target Training Group	Program Format	Program Objectives	Evaluation Criteria	Program Results
CalPERS Leadership Challenge	All levels	• Series of 3-day leadership workshops, conducted top-down • One-on-one private coaching • Creation of individual action plans	Produce positive, measurable change in leadership behavior	• 360-degree feedback instrument • Two 4-month survey progress assessments	• 90% reported improvement in leadership effectiveness over 4-month period • 87% indicated improvement over second 4-month period
Eastman Kodak Business Advantage Program	Professional Division, 400 leaders and executives	Customized business simulation	• Increased profitability • Better understanding of business and financial interrelationships • Improved financial performance	Participant reaction	• 98% rating program as very good or excellent • 64% stating that understanding and awareness of profitability influences increased by a "great extent" • Better understanding of impact of COGS on revenues and assets • $30 million inventory reduction on total delivered costs • $3 million process and inventory reductions • $500,000 asset reductions • $375,000 top line growth • Estimated $23.4 million return on $1.44 million investment; 16-to-1 ROI

Company	Target Training Group	Program Format	Program Objectives	Evaluation Criteria	Program Results
GM Service Parts Organization	• Senior faculty of pilot plant • Four control groups	• 2-day leadership assessment of senior faculty • Individual assessments • Customized LD program	• Improve SPO culture and business performance • Determine business impact of executive development	• Post-program survey • Anecdotal reports	• Managers and employees reported satisfaction with LD intervention • Pilot group productivity improved 21%; $4.4 million operating savings • ROI 15 to 1 • Increased health and safety • Lower absenteeism • Improved time management
IBM Accelerating Change Together (ACT) Initiative	• 300 internal consultants • Top executives	Instruction and application of ACT methodology	Achieving excellence through measurable results, sustainable change, and strong leadership capability		• $3.25 billion revenue growth • $1.2 billion productivity and overall client savings • $565 million inventory reduction • $3.75 billion market share growth Anecdotal: • Strengthened leadership • Faster, more disciplined implementation • Enhanced cross-business literacy • Improved knowledge management

(Continued)

Table 9.1. Continued.

Company	Target Training Group	Program Format	Program Objectives	Evaluation Criteria	Program Results
Siemens Nixdorf Information Systems AG: Entrepreneurial Development Program (EDP)	300 unit managers	Two 2-week segments with 6 to 8 weeks allotted in between for module work	• Identification, development, and capture of new business opportunities • Development of unit managers as corporate entrepreneurs • Development of general management skills • Help unit managers implement new business ventures	Business plan project	• Increased understanding of venture capital process • $250 million revenue increase from new client development
HP: Dynamic Leadership	8,000 managers	2 days, including instruction and group exercises, followed by 9 weeks on-the-job application	• Accelerate alignment to senior purpose • Improve collaboration across boundaries • Accelerate raising and resolving issues • Improve decision-making	• Post-program evaluations • Follow-through reports • Three-month post-program financial impact analysis	• 94% of participants reported using program tools in first 3 months after training, on average 9.5 times • $3,800 median value per reported application; 50% more than cost of program • ROI 15 to 1 • Reduced decision-making time and realignment with corporate goals • Improved customer service, higher quality, and better morale

Company	Target Training Group	Program Format	Program Objectives	Evaluation Criteria	Program Results
Capital One Coaching Initiative	Managers		• Capture full impact of coaching on performance • Determine value of coaching from within	Data captured from performance reviews of coaches, their peers, and their direct reports	• Majority of coaches outperformed peers • Direct reports of coaches received more favorable performance reviews, accelerated promotions
IBM Basic Blue Strategy	5,431 new managers		E-learning, on-the-job, and off-site development includes: • Weeklong classroom learning lab • 3 technology-delivered programs • Guided interactions around real business challenges • Business simulations • Individual exercises • Help new managers move into more complex roles • Equip managers to achieve IBM's business strategy • Align the organization around the business environment	Learning Management System (LMS) culls: • 360-degree feedback • Supervisor input • Participants' progress in online courses	• ROI: $450,000 per participant • 97% completion rate

APPENDIX A

EDA 2004 TRENDS SURVEY ADVISORY BOARD

Timothy T. Conlon
Chief Learning Officer and Corporate Director, Learning and Work Environment
Xerox Corporation
Conlon's responsibilities for Xerox include providing worldwide learning services and solutions, leadership assessment and development, and work environment research and survey processes.

Conlon received a master of business administration degree from the University of Rochester Simon School of Business.

Robert A. Gregory
Senior Consultant, Leadership Development, Western Hemisphere
BP America
Gregory is responsible for planning and implementation of needs analysis, planning, development, delivery, and evaluation of all learning programs. He serves as consultant, coach, and advisor to executives and managers on both individual development planning and development planning of their direct reports. He serves as a member of BP's Organizational and Individual Learning Network.

Gregory received a master's degree in counseling and a doctorate in psychology from the University of Tennessee.

Laura Mainville Guenther
Vice President of Learning
The ServiceMaster Companies

Guenther's primary responsibility is to lead enterprise-wide leadership development, focusing on improving performance in management and leadership ranks. She is also responsible for succession management and performance management at the senior levels in the organization.

Guenther received her master's degree in industrial organizational psychology from the University of Nebraska.

Alice Heezen
Group Management Development Manager
Rexam, PLC

Heezen runs Rexam's global business school, The Horizon Program, linking with some of the best business schools in the world to enhance Rexam's high-potential leadership capabilities.

Heezen received a master's degree in organizational and social psychology at Leiden University in the Netherlands.

Ashley Keith
Manager, Global Executive Development
Dell Inc.

Keith is responsible for developing and delivering the core curriculum to support Dell executives worldwide and for providing strategies and programs to develop the top talent.

She holds a bachelor's in psychology from the University of South Carolina and a master of science in organization development from the Johns Hopkins University.

Nancy J. Lewis
Vice President, IBM On Demand Learning

Lewis is responsible for IBM's leadership in learning design and development, learning systems, collaborative learning, and expertise. Her organization is focused on learning innovation and the effectiveness of IBM's top strategic learning initiatives. She created a new global management system for strategy and planning and has led a successful reengineering initiative to transform everything about the way that managers are developed at IBM.

Val H. Markos
Executive Director, Leadership Development
BellSouth Corporation
Markos is responsible for succession planning, high-potential development programs, and management education through the BellSouth Leadership Institute and staffing of the top 2 percent of positions in the company.

Markos holds a master of science and doctorate in industrial/organizational psychology.

Mary O'Hara
Vice President, People Development
Bell Canada Enterprises
O'Hara provides support and leadership to Bell Canada and BCE in the areas of talent management, enterprise learning, and personal development programs. Through partnerships with business leaders, her team develops strategies, programs, and tools to enhance and accelerate the leadership capacity in the organization and also increase functional and technical competence.

Currently pursuing a master's degree, she received her bachelor's degree from the University of Toronto's Rotman School of Business. She holds an honors diploma in human resource management.

Charles Presbury
Senior Director, Leadership Development
McGraw-Hill Companies, Inc.
Presbury is responsible for the design and implementation of key leadership development activities for McGraw-Hill. Specific areas include 360-degree feedback, curriculum design, and succession planning.

Presbury received a master's degree from Columbia University.

EDA 2004 TRENDS SURVEY RESPONDENT DEMOGRAPHICS

Among the 101 survey respondents

- Fifty-four percent have over $10 billion in revenues
- An additional 36 percent have over $1 billion in revenues
- Almost 17 percent have over 100,000 employees
- Over 60 percent have over 10,000 employees

Respondents are in these industry sectors:

- Manufacturing: 33 percent
- Information technology: 16.7 percent
- Communications technology: 15.7 percent
- Financial: 17.6 percent
- Services: 10.8 percent

Respondent companies are headquartered

- In the United States: 79 percent
- In Western Europe: 10 percent
- Elsewhere in the world: 11 percent

DEFINITIONS OF TWELVE BEST PRACTICES FROM THE EDA 2004 TRENDS SURVEY

In EDA's 2004 Trends Survey, respondents were asked to identify which of twelve executive development "best practices" they excelled in, based on the following definitions that we've provided:

Linked to strategy. Our executive development efforts are directly linked to our organization's strategy. It is clear how these efforts help address our marketplace challenges or achieve our strategic objectives.

Top management-driven. Our top executives champion our executive development efforts. We have a senior line executive advisory board. Our top executives attend the programs as participants and also teach when appropriate.

Strategy and system. We have a strategy and long-term plan for executive development. Our programs and practices are part of a continuous system and process, rather than stand-alone, ad hoc events.

Thorough front-end analysis. No significant executive development effort is begun without a thorough front-end or needs analysis.

Custom-designed. We custom-design our programs so that they address our unique, company-specific challenges and opportunities and help create or drive our vision, values, and strategies.

Leadership profile, feedback, and individual development plans. We use a custom-designed (linked to our vision, values, and strategies) multirater leadership instrument or inventory to provide confidential development feedback to our executives. Our executives have individual development plans based on that feedback.

Top-down implementation. Whenever our executive and leadership development efforts are aimed at organization change, our top management attends the programs first as participants. Then the programs are cascaded down throughout the organization.

Action-oriented learning. Our executive learning experiences are action oriented. Whenever feasible, we use some form of action learning in which participants apply what they are learning to real, current business problems and opportunities.

Succession management. We have an effective succession management system that ensures we have the right executive in the right job at the right time. We seldom are forced to hire from outside the organization to fill a key executive job opening because we don't have a qualified internal candidate prepared.

Integrated talent management system. We have a well-integrated talent management system (succession management, external and internal executive education, on-the-job development, coaching and mentoring, and so on) rather than independent, stand-alone processes.

Measurement. We set clear, measurable objectives when we create new executive development strategies, systems, processes, and programs. Then we measure the business impact using metrics that matter to senior management, and we communicate the results effectively.

High-potential identification and development. Our organization has an effective process for identifying high-potential talent and accelerating their development.

COMPARING 2000 AND 2004 TRENDS SURVEY RESULTS

Survey respondents chose the following as their top five concerns in response to selected questions on the 2000 and 2004 EDA Executive Development Trends Surveys.

Conditions that are highly influential on executive development:

2000

1. Changing business strategies
2. Demands of management
3. Increased competition
4. Changing corporate culture
5. Lack of benchstrength

2004

1. Lack of benchstrength
2. Changing business strategies
3. Increased competition
4. Increased collaboration across the organization
5. Globalization

Key objectives in executive development:

2000

1. Support strategic objectives
2. Address key business issues
3. Communicate vision/strategy
4. Increased benchstrength
5. Make talent a competitive advantage

2004

1. Increased benchstrength
2. Accelerate development of high-potentials
3. Communicate vision/strategy
4. Support change/transformation
5. Develop individual leader capabilities

Topics that will receive emphasis in executive development:

2000	*2004*
1. Leadership	1. Leadership
2. Strategy execution	2. Leading change
3. Leading change	3. Managing human performance
4. Strategy formulation	4. Strategy execution
5. Managing human performance	5. Business acumen

Policy and strategy activities that will be emphasized:

2000	*2004*
1. Integrated development system	1. Integrated development system
2. Integrated with HR system	2. Use of systematic measurement/ evaluation
3. Centralization of executive development	3. Integrated with HR system
4. Rewards for development	4. Creation of core curriculum
5. Use of advisory board	5. Creation of "milestone/transition" system

Planning and needs analysis methods:

2000	*2004*
1. Use of 360-degree results	1. Top management suggestions
2. Top management suggestions	2. Use of 360-degree results
3. Survey prospective users	3. Analysis of talent review results
4. Survey subordinates	4. Survey prospective users
5. Use steering committee	5. Formal performance/competency studies

Program design and development activities:

2000	*2004*
1. Researching new methods/ benchmarking	1. External design of courses by consultants
2. Internal design of courses	2. Internal design of courses
3. External design of courses by consultants	3. Researching new methods/ benchmarking
4. Systematic course evaluation	4. Systematic course evaluation
5. Internal staff training	5. Systematic measurement of ROI, business impact

Learning methods that will be emphasized:

2000	*2004*
1. Action learning	1. Senior executives as faculty
2. Outside experts	2. Action learning
3. Senior executives as teachers	3. Outside speakers
4. Outside speakers	4. Outside experts
5. Inside experts	5. External executive coaches

RESEARCH AND ANALYSIS: EXAMPLES OF DOCUMENTS TO GATHER AND REVIEW

Research and analysis is Step One of the five-step process for creating an executive development program described in Chapter Two. The following are examples of typical documents to gather and review in this step.

- Anything in writing about the project (that is, descriptions, objectives, copies of needs analyses already conducted and the results)
- Annual reports (stockholders and employees)
- 10K reports
- Statements of company strategy, mission, goals, values
- Company history
- Recent issues of company newsletter and videos
- Relevant organizational charts
- Anything that describes key markets and competition
- Product literature
- Key speeches made during the past few years
- Annual officer meeting agendas and minutes
- Analyst reports (reports by company officers to security analysts, outside analyst reports of the company)
- Copies of key human resource management documents (for example, appraisal forms, executive resource forms, incentive or bonus forms, and so on)

- Materials from formal new employee orientation program
- Descriptions of relevant existing or past management and executive training, education, or development programs and activities
- Aggregate 360-degree feedback data, performance appraisal data, talent reviews, and the like
- Recent employee surveys
- Customer-satisfaction surveys and focus group reports
- Climate, attitude, and engagement surveys
- Bios of executives to be interviewed
- Web site

APPENDIX F

DESIGN: TYPICAL ACTION-ORIENTED LEARNING ACTIVITIES

The following are typical learning activities to consider in an effective executive development program design:

- Case studies and discussions based on actual company situations
- Team projects based on real business challenges (action learning)
- Team workshops
- Presentations
- Self-assessment
- Action planning
- Custom business simulations
- Adventure learning
- Interactive lectures
- The Leader's Court
- Orienteering
- Benchmarking other organizations
- Community projects—for example, Habitat for Humanity
- Peer feedback
- 360-degree feedback

APPENDIX G

PILOT PROGRAM: TYPICAL FACILITATOR ACTIVITIES

The following are typical facilitator activities that an executive development program facilitator might engage in, to consider including:

- Program overview (for example, history, objectives, program design, flow, overall content, and so on)
- Icebreaking exercises
- Participant introductions
- Overview of each module, including objectives, process, and fit with program content
- Bridging between modules regarding how they fit or relate
- Introducing faculty
- Teaching (if appropriate)
- Preparing, evaluating, and coaching faculty as needed
- Moderating panels and workshops
- Coaching subgroups on effective meeting and problem-solving skills
- Assisting participants in summarizing key learnings
- Evaluating program effectiveness and conducting debriefings with program manager and top management
- Reporting to top management on progress and recommending actions

APPENDIX H

EDA'S RAPID-CYCLE DESIGN® PROCESS

As noted in Chapter Two, EDA's five-step process usually takes about six months to complete. Clients have expressed concerns that the process is, in some cases, too slow, and that they are having trouble securing ownership or buy-in from the company's line management.

An issue we've experienced while designing programs is the sponsor's insistence on the *perfect* solution. So much emphasis is placed on the design of a program—which is bound to change after the pilot program stage—that the exorbitant time investment hardly justifies the return.

In response, we developed our Rapid-Cycle Design® Process (RCD) to simultaneously

- Streamline the five-step process, dramatically reducing the time to market for new strategies and programs
- Engage key line executives in a way that results in their ownership of the new executive development strategy and programs

RCD takes into account the need to abbreviate the preparation by adjusting the focus somewhat from the quality of the initial design (Q) to the acceptance (A) of a development program. Look at it this way: a company that spends a good deal of time designing a program, without enlisting any buy-in, is severely reducing the value of that program. Yet if the program engages line executives earlier in the process, the potential effectiveness of that program increases, even if the original design quality of the program might be somewhat lower. Figure H.1 illustrates this point.

If the typical perfectionist's take on a quality design (Q) equals 0.99 and acceptance of the program (A) is low—say, 0.20—the effectiveness quotient (E) is compromised.

If Q x A= E, then (0.99) x (0.20) = (0.19), where 0.19 represents effectiveness. However, if you gain acceptance of your program in the initial stages of the process, you significantly increase your effectiveness. If, say, your quality design (Q) equals 0.70 and acceptance of the program (A) is higher—say, 0.80—your effectiveness quotient (E) increases: (0.70) x (0.80) = (0.56), where 0.56 represents increased effectiveness. That's the outcome of the Rapid-Cycle Design® Process.

How is this shift to increased acceptance implemented? By modifying the first two steps of the five-step process (first, research and analysis, and second, design, as described in Chapter Two) with enhanced steps that speed up the process and increase line management engagement.

Rapid-Cycle Diagnostics^SM

This diagnostics process is designed to reduce the length of the needs assessment process and increase engagement in your executive development program. At the

Figure H.1. An A+ Implementation of a B+ Idea = Faster Impact.

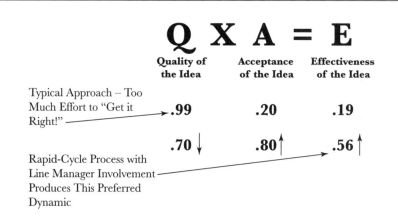

heart of this approach is a web-based executive-level needs assessment that can be tailored to an organization's unique situation.

The web-based needs assessment can be created, implemented, and analyzed in a fraction of the time it takes to interview a typical 15-percent sample of the target audience. This approach also makes it practical to reach many more people at minimal incremental cost. This provides the potential advantage of engaging everyone in the target audience and therefore increasing the level of buy-in to the end product.

The thought of engaging all key stakeholders may seem far-fetched, but our experience with this has been entirely positive. While developing the Weyerhaeuser Leadership Institute (Chapter Seven), for example, participants were initially resistant to filling out "another survey." So we asked the business unit leaders to send the survey only to those they thought should take the time to review it, and we made completion of the survey optional. Most of the unit leaders ended up sending it to all of their executives. Much to their surprise, they received completed responses from about half of them—most of them with considerable write-in comments. The survey takes about thirty minutes to complete. In our experience, response rates are typically 50 percent at the executive level. One company we worked with achieved an 80-percent response rate.

Rapid-Cycle Diagnostics comprises four critical components: strategic review, web-based survey, executive interviews, and findings.

Strategic Review

The goal of this component is understanding the background of the business and its challenges so that the Rapid-Cycle Diagnostics methods can be tailored and focused. This involves reviewing much of the data and information required in Step One of the five-step process described in Chapter Two (see Appendix E for suggested documents to review).

Web-Based Survey

This brief thirty-minute survey is customized and made easily accessible on any common internet browser (Figure H.2 shows an excerpt from such a survey). Key stakeholders are asked questions whose answers allow the development team to do the following:

- Assess their understanding and alignment around vision and strategy
- Identify their organization's critical marketplace and organizational challenges
- Identify organizational capabilities needed to meet those challenges

Figure H.2. Executive Development Needs Analysis.

Introduction

This survey explores the business and leadership challenges of your organization and the leadership developement capabilities needed to successfully address those challenges. Your responses are anonymous and will be combined with the responses of other executives. You will need about 30 minutes to complete this form.

Begin by answering a few questions about your organization in general, its challenges, strengths and vulnerabilities. For the purpose of these questions, define the organization as the total enterprise overall (not just your area).

1. **In your opinion, which of the following marketplace challenges and changes will have an impact on the organization in the next few years? For each item, indicate whether you believe it will have no impact, a small impact, a substantial impact or a huge impact on the organization.**

	No Impact	Small Impact	Substantial Impact	Huge Impact
More competitors	O	O	O	O
Improved quality of competition	O	O	O	O
More globalization	O	O	O	O
More demanding customers	O	O	O	O
More sophisticated customers	O	O	O	O
Mergers and acquisitions	O	O	O	O
Strategic alliances and partnerships	O	O	O	O
Shorter product life cycles	O	O	O	O

- Identify executive and leadership capabilities needed to address the company's marketplace challenges, achieve its vision, execute its strategy, and live its values (see Appendix I for examples)

Executive Interviews

These are a more abbreviated version of the interviews conducted in the five-step process (that is, there are fewer interviews). This step is designed as a follow-up to the web-based survey. It clarifies survey findings and obtains top leaders' input and reactions to the survey results. Questions usually address such topics as these:

- The business environment and its implications
- Marketplace and business challenges
- Vision, strategy, values
- Executive and leadership capability gaps
- Reactions to the preliminary Web-based survey findings

Findings

The combination of the Web-based needs assessment and interviews (Diagnostics) helps determine the development needs and priorities needed to move on to the core element, the RCD Workshop.

Rapid-Cycle Design Workshop

The RCD Workshop replaces Step Two of the five-step process, the design step, and engages line executives in defining the specific priorities and processes to be included in an executive development strategy and program. In this way, the RCD Workshop uses the organizational development concept of "no involvement, no commitment."

The RCD Workshop comprises three key components: preparation, the workshop, and sponsor review and input.

Preparation

Workshop participants are sometimes invited to use a Web site to prepare them for the workshop and ensure that everyone begins with the same level of understanding. The site should help them to

- Develop an understanding of the project context, purpose, and objectives
- Review findings from Web-based needs assessment and interviews
- Provide presession reading materials on best practices in executive development

The Workshop

The workshop brings line executives and human resources together in the work of converting the company's business needs into a strong executive development strategy and program design. The workshop typically lasts three days, with the line executives involved in the first two days.

In the first two days the following activities take place with the line executives (see Figure H.3 for a graphical presentation):

The workshop opens with a briefing by the CEO on the importance of the project and the company vision, strategy, and critical priorities. This is done first so that everything is grounded in the needs and realities of the business.

External speakers or guest faculty are asked to provide insight regarding trends in the industry. This enables participants to compare their company and better identify the relevant business context for the executive development effort.

Participants analyze the findings from the diagnostics step. The goal is for the line executives to wrestle with the findings—including the Web-based survey—and identify, agree on, and prioritize the company's executive development needs.

An EDA consultant or other expert on trends and best practices in the executive development field opens the workshop with a briefing on executive

Figure H.3. EDA Rapid-Cycle Design: Typical Process.

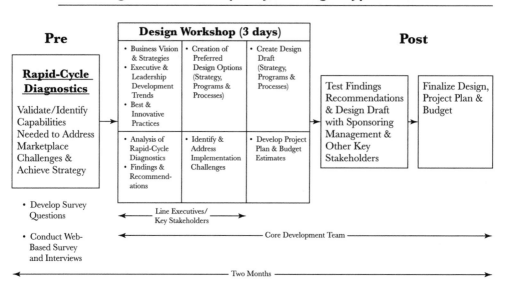

development trends and best practices. This serves to broaden and deepen the knowledge base of participants, enabling them to think beyond their personal experience and be more creative. In a way, it's also preparing them to do their job of translating the executive development needs they've identified into high-level executive development strategy and program design ideas.

High-level design options and guidelines are created. This typically starts with the presentation of relevant design concepts and ideas from other organizations so that the participants have some suggestions to consider before they start their design work. After all, they aren't experts in executive development, so it's not realistic for them to start with a blank sheet of paper. They will go on to create high-level design concepts, themes, objectives, and preferred learning methods that fit with the company culture, and identify the target groups and required resources.

• Finally, we ask line executives to identify likely challenges they will face during implementation and to brainstorm how to overcome those challenges.

Throughout the two days, we coach the teams and act as consultants and subject matter experts along with the internal executive development staff. On the third day, after the line executives have departed, the project team (typically, the core company executive development team and our consultants) synthesizes the work output from the previous two days. They then collaborate in the creation of (1) a more detailed design (strategy, architecture, programs, objectives, agendas, learning methods, and so on) to meet the company's identified needs; (2) a project plan for development of the strategy, processes, and programs; and (3) a budget.

Sponsor Review and Input

It is obviously essential to the process to develop both support for the recommendations and a commitment of resources to implement them. This ensures that the proposed direction is in alignment with the company's strategic objectives, and it provides another opportunity to obtain input and build ownership. This step also builds the momentum needed to execute the program. Usually this means presenting the output from the workshop to the CEO and senior leadership team members for final review and approval.

The research and analysis and design processes, as outlined in the five-step process (Chapter Two), can take six months to complete; the RCD process completes the same work in two months or less. While the longer process provides some qualitative advantages, the significant speed-to-market and line ownership advantages of RCD are making it the preferred methodology of many clients.

Once the RCD Workshop process is complete, the remaining three steps of the five-step process can be implemented: Step Three, material development and faculty sourcing; Step Four, pilot program; and Step Five, follow-through and continuous improvement (see Chapter Two).

Outcomes You Can Expect from the Rapid-Cycle Design Process

At the conclusion of the RCD process, the executive development design team should have the following:

- Enhanced understanding of the marketplace challenges and business vision, strategy and objectives
- The executive capabilities required to successfully address marketplace challenges and achieve business objectives
- Prioritized executive development needs
- An executive development strategy to address these needs
- Specific program designs to support the strategy
- A customized 360-degree leadership feedback instrument[1]
- Identification of implementation issues and ways to ensure organizational support for the development strategy, system, and programs

1. This is a newly developed instrument if one did not already exist; if one did, it is recalibrated.

- Line leaders dedicated to the implementation of the executive development plans
- Champions within the company who are eager and willing to serve as ongoing advisors, that is, on an advisory board or steering committee

We've found the outcomes and benefits of these specific processes to be far superior to others conducted without this serious engagement of line leaders. They create thorough due diligence and buy-in on the part of key stakeholders, as well as a customized approach—which we see as the most effective way to build the capabilities needed to achieve the organization's strategy.

APPENDIX I

WEB-BASED SURVEY:
TYPICAL QUESTION THEMES

The following are common themes for questions included in a Web-based survey that stakeholders complete for use by the design and development team:

- The most significant marketplace challenges facing the company and the implications for the organization and its leaders
- The vision and key strategies required to achieve that vision
- The organization's strengths and weaknesses
- The current culture and values and how they must change in order to fully achieve the vision and successfully execute the strategy
- The executive/leadership capabilities (mindsets, knowledge, and skills) of the typical leader or executive today
- The biggest gaps between existing executive and leadership capabilities and those needed to achieve the vision, live the values, and execute the strategy
- Topics you would want to see included to build the capabilities the company needs to win in the marketplace today and in the future
- Topics that would be most useful to you personally
- Preferred learning methods based on past developmental experiences

DIFFERENT WAYS OF MEASURING EXECUTIVE DEVELOPMENT

The ways of measuring the impact of executive development efforts are of course as varied as the companies that make such efforts. Here's a summary of what can be learned about metrics in their many forms, based on the case studies in Chapter Nine.

Anecdotal Evidence

We often turn up our noses at anecdotal evidence. But for many CEOs and other senior leaders, this is the gold standard. Sometimes it's the only thing they care about.

Anecdotal evidence ranges from what you hear in the hallways—the "buzz" about it, what participants are saying to other employees about the executive development experience they've had—to the end-of-program "smile sheets"— what participants write on evaluation forms at the end of a program, process, or event. Such feedback is, of course, highly valuable, and should be summarized and communicated to all key stakeholders. At the same time, it's the least reliable from a scientific standpoint, so it shouldn't be relied upon as the sole source of measurement.

Follow-Up Evaluations

We almost always send out post-program or post-process evaluations two to six months after a program has ended. Typically we make three simple requests on one side of one sheet of paper:

1. Please describe one thing you learned that you have applied on the job.
2. Please describe the effect it had on your performance or the performance of your team or your organization.
3. If there has been a quantifiable impact (such as on costs, revenues, or profits) that you've experienced or expect, please describe.

It's amazing what valuable information you can get from this simple effort. For example, in the first Weyerhaeuser Leadership Institute (see Chapter Seven), the financial results were close to a billion dollars from a combination of increased sales, cost savings, and productivity gains. This figure was so high that the head of strategic education was concerned that the actual financial results were so staggering that the senior team would not believe them. He decided to report only 10 percent of the results to be sure senior executives would find it credible.

Readministration of the 360-Degree Leadership Inventory

Many companies have found this to be the best available way to measure improvements in leadership effectiveness, at both the individual and the organizational levels. Readministering the 360-degree leadership inventory six months or more after the end of a program allows us to measure improvements in leadership effectiveness as perceived by direct reports, peers, and the manager.

This is a highly flexible tool. It allows you to measure improvements in leadership effectiveness at the individual, team, function, business unit, and enterprise levels. As an additional benefit, the aggregate results can also serve as a needs assessment.

For example, when we helped BellSouth with its new Leadership Institute architecture and initial program, the aggregate feedback from the top three hundred executives' 360-degree feedback allowed us to identify the common low scores and use these to determine the objectives and content for the second Leadership Institute program.

Control Groups

As you can see from several of the cases, it is certainly possible to compare groups of people who have received development with those who have not and to identify the differences in their performance. You can compare their average performance appraisal ratings, comparative business results, and so on.

Action Learning Projects

Whenever you use action learning (working on real business problems or opportunities in teams for development purposes) you have a pretty easy way to measure the impact. Was the project completed? Were the project objectives achieved? Were the project recommendations implemented? If so, did they achieve the intended business impact?

You need to clearly specify your expected outcomes for a project if you hope to measure improvements later on. This is demonstrated by the IBM ACT case study in Chapter Nine. All the ACT projects had hard business outcomes specified up front, which made them very easy to measure.

Return on Investment (ROI)

A couple of the companies measured ROI in a fairly classic way. They calculated the entire cost of running the executive or leadership program—including the development costs, travel, hotel, time off the job, and so on—and compared this figure against all the recorded financial results. This is how HP and Kodak came up with their ROI figures of fifteen to one.

We still face the challenge of finding new and better metrics. As professionals in the field, we think it would be negligent not to do so.

Index

ABOUT THE AUTHORS

James F. Bolt

Jim Bolt is chairman and founder of Executive Development Associates, Inc., (EDA), a leading consulting firm specializing in the strategic use of executive development. Prior to founding EDA, Jim was with Xerox Corporation for over sixteen years. As corporate director of human resource planning and development, he had worldwide responsibility for executive education, leadership development, and succession management. Earlier in his Xerox career, Jim held several key line positions.

Jim was recently selected by the *Financial Times* as one of the top experts in executive and leadership development. Linkage, Inc., named him one of the top fifty executive coaches in the world.

Jim is the author of the book *Executive Development: A Strategy for Corporate Competitiveness*. He has contributed to several books on leadership and executive development and human resources, including a chapter on "Developing Three-Dimensional Leaders" in the Peter F. Drucker Foundation book *The Leader of the Future*. He has authored more than twenty articles, including "Tailor Executive Development to Strategy," published in the *Harvard Business Review*.

Jim's most recent published work includes:

- "Learning at the Top: How CEOs Set the Tone for the Knowledge Organization" in *Leading Organizational Learning* (Jossey-Bass, 2004)
- "Coaching for Leadership Development" in *Profiles in Coaching* (Linkage, Inc., 2004)
- "Develop Your Top Executives Through a Participative 'Rapid-Cycle' Design Process" in *The Change Champions Field Guide* (BPI, 2003)

Jim can be reached at jbolt@executivedevelopment.com.

Michael Dulworth

Mike Dulworth, managing director of EDA, specializes in helping organizations achieve significant improvements in performance through the utilization of innovative business practices supported by web-enabled technologies. Mike has twenty years' experience working with government institutions, not-for-profit organizations, and Fortune 1000 companies to develop e-business strategies; assess organizational needs and readiness; design, develop, and implement organizational development interventions; create technology-based learning systems; and measure operational performance outcomes. His approach is built on a deep understanding of organizational behavior and culture, change management, business systems, organization and individual assessment, performance measurement, web technologies, and systems design, development, and deployment.

Before joining EDA, Mike was a vice president at The Concours Group, responsible for the firm's learning services practice. Prior to that, he was chairman and CEO of Learning Technologies Group, Inc. (LTG). LTG won the Gold Medal for Online Training from the *NewMedia Invision Awards* in 1999.

Mike has also held senior positions at Insync Corporation, The Conference Board, Sirota & Alper Associates, and the U.S. General Accounting Office. He was named one of the Top 100 multimedia producers by *AV/Multimedia Producer* magazine in 1998, and Insync was awarded the HR Product of the Year Award by *HR Executive* magazine in 1991. Mike has a BA from the University of Michigan and an MPA, with a concentration in organizational behavior, from the University of Southern California.

Mike can be reached at mdulworth@executivedevelopment.com.

Michael R. McGrath

Michael McGrath, vice president, consulting at EDA, has worked for over twenty-five years in executive and organizational development. Prior to EDA, he was vice-president, executive education and development at Charles Schwab & Co., Inc., where he was responsible for the talent portfolio planning and development process for the firm's top two hundred executives, including creating and implementing the succession planning process for the senior management team; coaching members of the executive committee and members of their senior team in executive and leadership development; and the design, delivery, and launch of the core executive leadership development programs.

Previously, as an internal change agent, Michael served as head of organization development at Rockwell Semiconductor Products Businesses, supporting the senior team on a two-year business turnaround. As an external consultant, Michael has worked with senior executive teams (such as those of Cisco, Raychem, Fluor Daniel, Johnson Controls, and Rockwell International) on both individual executive effectiveness and senior team performance.

Michael served as senior vice president for Personnel Decisions International (PDI), for which he founded the San Francisco office. He helped grow it into a full-service operating office providing executive education and development, assessment, executive coaching, 360-degree feedback and development planning, and organizational effectiveness services.

Michael taught at both the University of Michigan and University of Southern California (USC). At the University of Michigan, he worked as part of the Ford Motor Company Leadership Development program; this gave him the opportunity to coach hundreds of global Ford executives around aligning their personal development with Ford's strategic imperatives. He also served as an assistant professor of management and organization at the Graduate School of Business at USC.

Michael earned his doctorate in organizational behavior and his master's degree in public administration (human resources and organization development) from Rockefeller College of Public Affairs and Policy, State University of New York at Albany. He earned his bachelor's in American studies from Siena College.

Michael can be reached at mmcgrath@executivedevelopment.com.

About Executive Development Associates, Inc.

EDA develops custom-designed executive development strategies, systems, and programs that ensure clients have the executive talent needed to achieve their strategic objectives. EDA's clients have included half of the Fortune 100 companies and many other leading organizations around the world. EDA clientele include AT&T, Aventis Pharmaceuticals, Bell Canada, Charles Schwab, Dell Inc., Coca-Cola, Colgate-Palmolive, GE, Hewlett-Packard, IBM, Johnson & Johnson, Mitsubishi, Motorola, Save The Children, San Miguel Corporation, Sun Microsystems, Texas Instruments, The New York Stock Exchange, UBS, and Weyerhaeuser.

EDA exists to ensure that an organization's executive talent is a competitive advantage, through these services:

- Creating high-impact, custom-designed executive development strategies, systems, and programs
- Developing customized executive talent strategies and integrated systems
- Supporting the success and effectiveness of executives through a powerful community of practice networks
- Conducting research that advances the state of the art and is also practical and immediately applicable

San Francisco Headquarters:
225 Bush St., Suite 770
San Francisco, CA 94104
Phone: (415) 399-9797
Fax: (415) 399-9696

New York Office:
230 Park Avenue, 10th floor
New York, NY 10169
Phone: (212) 551-3617
Fax: (212) 808-3020
Contact EDA at eda@executivedevelopment.com
www.executivedevelopment.com

Pfeiffer Publications Guide

This guide is designed to familiarize you with the various types of Pfeiffer publications. The formats section describes the various types of products that we publish; the methodologies section describes the many different ways that content might be provided within a product. We also provide a list of the topic areas in which we publish.

FORMATS

In addition to its extensive book-publishing program, Pfeiffer offers content in an array of formats, from fieldbooks for the practitioner to complete, ready-to-use training packages that support group learning.

FIELDBOOK Designed to provide information and guidance to practitioners in the midst of action. Most fieldbooks are companions to another, sometimes earlier, work, from which its ideas are derived; the fieldbook makes practical what was theoretical in the original text. Fieldbooks can certainly be read from cover to cover. More likely, though, you'll find yourself bouncing around following a particular theme, or dipping in as the mood, and the situation, dictate.

HANDBOOK A contributed volume of work on a single topic, comprising an eclectic mix of ideas, case studies, and best practices sourced by practitioners and experts in the field.

An editor or team of editors usually is appointed to seek out contributors and to evaluate content for relevance to the topic. Think of a handbook not as a ready-to-eat meal, but as a cookbook of ingredients that enables you to create the most fitting experience for the occasion.

RESOURCE Materials designed to support group learning. They come in many forms: a complete, ready-to-use exercise (such as a game); a comprehensive resource on one topic (such as conflict management) containing a variety of methods and approaches; or a collection of like-minded activities (such as icebreakers) on multiple subjects and situations.

TRAINING PACKAGE An entire, ready-to-use learning program that focuses on a particular topic or skill. All packages comprise a guide for the facilitator/trainer and a workbook for the participants. Some packages are supported with additional media—such as video—or learning aids, instruments, or other devices to help participants understand concepts or practice and develop skills.

- *Facilitator/trainer's guide* Contains an introduction to the program, advice on how to organize and facilitate the learning event, and step-by-step instructor notes. The guide also contains copies of presentation materials—handouts, presentations, and overhead designs, for example—used in the program.

• *Participant's workbook* Contains exercises and reading materials that support the learning goal and serves as a valuable reference and support guide for participants in the weeks and months that follow the learning event. Typically, each participant will require his or her own workbook.

ELECTRONIC CD-ROMs and web-based products transform static Pfeiffer content into dynamic, interactive experiences. Designed to take advantage of the searchability, automation, and ease-of-use that technology provides, our e-products bring convenience and immediate accessibility to your workspace.

METHODOLOGIES

CASE STUDY A presentation, in narrative form, of an actual event that has occurred inside an organization. Case studies are not prescriptive, nor are they used to prove a point; they are designed to develop critical analysis and decision-making skills. A case study has a specific time frame, specifies a sequence of events, is narrative in structure, and contains a plot structure—an issue (what should be/have been done?). Use case studies when the goal is to enable participants to apply previously learned theories to the circumstances in the case, decide what is pertinent, identify the real issues, decide what should have been done, and develop a plan of action.

ENERGIZER A short activity that develops readiness for the next session or learning event. Energizers are most commonly used after a break or lunch to stimulate or refocus the group. Many involve some form of physical activity, so they are a useful way to counter post-lunch lethargy. Other uses include transitioning from one topic to another, where "mental" distancing is important.

EXPERIENTIAL LEARNING ACTIVITY (ELA) A facilitator-led intervention that moves participants through the learning cycle from experience to application (also known as a Structured Experience). ELAs are carefully thought-out designs in which there is a definite learning purpose and intended outcome. Each step—everything that participants do during the activity—facilitates the accomplishment of the stated goal. Each ELA includes complete instructions for facilitating the intervention and a clear statement of goals, suggested group size and timing, materials required, an explanation of the process, and, where appropriate, possible variations to the activity. (For more detail on Experiential Learning Activities, see the Introduction to the *Reference Guide to Handbooks and Annuals*, 1999 edition, Pfeiffer, San Francisco.)

GAME A group activity that has the purpose of fostering team spirit and togetherness in addition to the achievement of a pre-stated goal. Usually contrived—undertaking a desert expedition, for example—this type of learning method offers an engaging means for participants to demonstrate and practice business and interpersonal skills. Games are effective for team building and personal development mainly because the goal is subordinate to the process—the means through which participants reach decisions, collaborate, communicate, and generate trust and understanding. Games often engage teams in "friendly" competition.

ICEBREAKER A (usually) short activity designed to help participants overcome initial anxiety in a training session and/or to acquaint the participants with one another. An icebreaker can be a fun activity or can be tied to specific topics or training goals. While a useful tool in itself, the icebreaker comes into its own in situations where tension or resistance exists within a group.

INSTRUMENT A device used to assess, appraise, evaluate, describe, classify, and summarize various aspects of human behavior. The term used to describe an instrument depends primarily on its format and purpose. These terms include survey, questionnaire, inventory, diagnostic, survey, and poll. Some uses of instruments include providing instrumental feedback to group members, studying here-and-now processes or functioning within a group, manipulating group composition, and evaluating outcomes of training and other interventions.

Instruments are popular in the training and HR field because, in general, more growth can occur if an individual is provided with a method for focusing specifically on his or her own behavior. Instruments also are used to obtain information that will serve as a basis for change and to assist in workforce planning efforts.

Paper-and-pencil tests still dominate the instrument landscape with a typical package comprising a facilitator's guide, which offers advice on administering the instrument and interpreting the collected data, and an initial set of instruments. Additional instruments are available separately. Pfeiffer, though, is investing heavily in e-instruments. Electronic instrumentation provides effortless distribution and, for larger groups particularly, offers advantages over paper-and-pencil tests in the time it takes to analyze data and provide feedback.

LECTURETTE A short talk that provides an explanation of a principle, model, or process that is pertinent to the participants' current learning needs. A lecturette is intended to establish a common language bond between the trainer and the participants by providing a mutual frame of reference. Use a lecturette as an introduction to a group activity or event, as an interjection during an event, or as a handout.

MODEL A graphic depiction of a system or process and the relationship among its elements. Models provide a frame of reference and something more tangible, and more easily remembered, than a verbal explanation. They also give participants something to "go on," enabling them to track their own progress as they experience the dynamics, processes, and relationships being depicted in the model.

ROLE PLAY A technique in which people assume a role in a situation/scenario: a customer service rep in an angry-customer exchange, for example. The way in which the role is approached is then discussed and feedback is offered. The role play is often repeated using a different approach and/or incorporating changes made based on feedback received. In other words, role playing is a spontaneous interaction involving realistic behavior under artificial (and safe) conditions.

SIMULATION A methodology for understanding the interrelationships among components of a system or process. Simulations differ from games in that they test or use a model that depicts or mirrors some aspect of reality in form, if not necessarily in content. Learning occurs by studying the effects of change on one or more factors of the model. Simulations are commonly used to test hypotheses about what happens in a system—often referred to as "what if?" analysis—or to examine best-case/worst-case scenarios.

THEORY A presentation of an idea from a conjectural perspective. Theories are useful because they encourage us to examine behavior and phenomena through a different lens.

TOPICS

The twin goals of providing effective and practical solutions for workforce training and organization development and meeting the educational needs of training and human resource professionals shape Pfeiffer's publishing program. Core topics include the following:

Leadership & Management

Communication & Presentation

Coaching & Mentoring

Training & Development

E-Learning

Teams & Collaboration

OD & Strategic Planning

Human Resources

Consulting

What will you find on pfeiffer.com?

• The best in workplace performance solutions for training and HR professionals

• Downloadable training tools, exercises, and content

• Web-exclusive offers

• Training tips, articles, and news

• Seamless on-line ordering

• Author guidelines, information on becoming a Pfeiffer Affiliate, and much more

Discover more at www.pfeiffer.com

Customer Care

Have a question, comment, or suggestion? Contact us! We value your feedback and we want to hear from you.

For questions about this or other Pfeiffer products, you may contact us by:

E-mail: **customer@wiley.com**

Mail: **Customer Care Wiley/Pfeiffer**
        10475 Crosspoint Blvd.
        Indianapolis, IN 46256

Phone: **(US) 800-274-4434** (Outside the US: 317-572-3985)

Fax: **(US) 800-569-0443** (Outside the US: 317-572-4002)

To order additional copies of this title or to browse other Pfeiffer products, visit us online at **www.pfeiffer.com**.

For **Technical Support** questions call **(800) 274-4434.**

For authors guidelines, log on to www.pfeiffer.com and click on "Resources for Authors."

If you are . . .

A **college bookstore, a professor, an instructor, or work in higher education** and you'd like to place an order or request an exam copy, please contact jbreview@wiley.com.

A **general retail bookseller** and you'd like to establish an account or speak to a local sales representative, contact Melissa Grecco at 201-748-6267 or mgrecco@wiley.com.

An **exclusively on-line bookseller**, contact Amy Blanchard at 530-756-9456 or ablanchard @wiley.com or Jennifer Johnson at 206-568-3883 or jjohnson@wiley.com, both of our Online Sales department.

A **librarian or library representative**, contact John Chambers in our Library Sales department at 201-748-6291 or jchamber@wiley.com.

A **reseller, training company/consultant, or corporate trainer**, contact Charles Regan in our Special Sales department at 201-748-6553 or cregan@wiley.com.

A **specialty retail distributor** (includes specialty gift stores, museum shops, and corporate bulk sales), contact Kim Hendrickson in our Special Sales department at 201-748-6037 or khendric@wiley.com.

Purchasing for the **Federal government**, contact Ron Cunningham in our Special Sales department at 317-572-3053 or rcunning@wiley.com.

Purchasing for a **State or Local government**, contact Charles Regan in our Special Sales department at 201-748-6553 or cregan@wiley.com.